Philipp Freiherr von Boeselager

Valkyrie

Philipp Freiherr von Boeselager was born in Bonn, Germany, in 1917, the fifth of nine children. He was raised with a liberal education, strong moral and religious values, and a love of hunting. In 1938, he enlisted and was placed in the cavalry regiment. He rose to the rank of commanding lieutenant, only to join the German resistance in 1941. His participation in Valkyrie went undetected, and he lived to be the last surviving member of the plot. In 2003, France awarded von Boeselager the Legion of Honor. He died on May 1, 2008.

Florence Fehrenbach is the granddaughter of Karl von Wendt, a coconspirator and close friend of Philipp von Boeselager. She and her husband, Jérôme Fehrenbach, convinced Boeselager, at the age of eighty-nine, to recount his experience.

VALKYRIE

Valkyrie

The Story of the Plot to Kill Hitler,
by Its Last Member

Philipp Freiherr von Boeselager

WITH FLORENCE AND JÉRÔME FEHRENBACH

Translated from the French by Steven Rendall

Vintage Books
A Division of Random House, Inc.
New York

FIRST VINTAGE BOOKS EDITION, JUNE 2010

Translation copyright © 2009 by Weidenfeld & Nicholson

All images are from the author's personal collection, with the exception of three images: January 1942 image inside Hitler's headquarters at Rastenburg, East Prussia, © Ullstein Bild; July 9, 2004, image of Philipp von Boeselager © AFP (Agence France-Presse); July 20, 2004, image of Philipp with his wife, Rosy, © AFP (Agence France-Presse).

The Library of Congress has cataloged the Knopf edition as follows:
Boeselager, Philipp Leopold Antonius Hubertus, Freiherr von, 1917–2008.
[Nous voulions tuer Hitler. English]
Valkyrie / Philipp Freiherr von Boeselager with Florence and Jérôme
Fehrenbach ; translated by Steven Rendall.—1st American ed.
p. cm.
Originally published: Paris : Perrin, c2008, under title Nous voulions tuer Hitler : le dernier survivant du complot du 20 juillet 1944.
Includes bibliographical references.
1. Hitler, Adolf, 1889–1945—Assassination attempt, 1944 (July 20). 2. Germany—Politics and government—1933–1945. 3. Conspiracies—Germany—History—20th century. 4. Boeselager, Philipp Leopold Antonius Hebertus, Freiherr von, 1917–2008. 5. Soldiers—Germany—Biography. I. Fehrenbach, Florence. II. Fehrenbach, Jérôme. III. Title.
DD256.35.B6413 2009
943.086'4092—dc22
[B] 2008055539

Vintage ISBN: 978-0-307-45497-3

Author photograph © AFP (Agence France-Presse)
Book design by Peter A. Andersen

www.vintagebooks.com

To my comrades in the Tresckow group,
who made their motto

Etiam si omnes, ego non!

Contents

	Foreword	ix
1.	*A Taste for Freedom*	3
2.	*The Time of Choices* (1933–36)	12
3.	*The Phony War* (1939–40)	25
4.	*A Dive for Victory* (June 9, 1940)	27
5.	*A Promise* (June 17, 1940)	31
6.	*A Lightning Campaign* (June–November 1941)	35
7.	*A Christmas in Hell* (December 1941–	
	January 1942)	46
8.	*The Conspiracy Begins* (1941–42)	60
9.	*An Encounter with the Demon* (June 1942)	71
10.	*An Incident at the Führer's*	
	Headquarters (July 1942)	84
11.	*A Poisoned Gift* (October 1942)	89
12.	*The Tresckow Group* (1942–44)	95
13.	*When Horses Make Meetings Easier* (1943)	105
14.	*The Three Failed Attempts* (March 1943)	113
15.	*Stopping the Barbarians*	122
16.	*Cavalrymen in Torment*	125
17.	*The Valise Full of Explosives*	140

Contents

18. *Obligatory Inactivity*   143
19. *The Dangerous Ride* (July 1944)   149
20. *A Time for Mourning*   163
21. *The Bridge over the Mura* (1945)   176
     Epilogue   184
     Afterword   189
     Notes   193
     Bibliography   199
     Illustration Credits   201
     Index   203

Foreword

Philipp von Boeselager is a rare person. He can provide testimony about his experience and development that is precious for our time. That is the purpose of this book.

Were it not for a few traces of the wounds he received in combat, one would never guess that this old man who radiates an impression of inner peace experienced the interminable nightmare of the Second World War—and especially, that he lived in a state of perpetual anxiety resulting from his participation in the conspiracies against Hitler. To be a conspirator was to plan a crime. In the eyes of other Germans, it was to betray one's country and hasten its final destruction. It was, finally, to carry on a double life, a difficult task for a man who had been brought up only to be a horseman.

To mention Philipp von Boeselager here without also mentioning his brother Georg would make no sense. They were inseparable in their childhood games and in the rigors of the war, and they both carried the secret of the conspiracy. No doubt they did so out of a sense of duty, a way of being and thinking that is illustrated by an episode — anecdotal with respect to history — that will be recounted in the afterword.

Von Boeselager agreed to participate in long conversations about the period that provided the subject matter for this book. He does not like to talk about these matters. Every reference to them elicits memories that are almost always painful. Even after the war, his participation in the plots against Hitler was a difficult secret to bear. At first he did not even share this with his wife. But he is the last one of the conspirators who is still alive, and since Boeselager does not believe in chance, he knows that he has survived in order to testify.

Florence and Jérôme Fehrenbach
Saint-Chaffrey, France,
August 16, 2007

VALKYRIE

1

A Taste for Freedom

My brother Georg was born in August 1915, I in September 1917. We were the fourth and fifth in a family of nine children.

My family had settled in Heimerzheim, in the Rhineland, in 1910, leaving our old home in Bonn, which in the eighteenth century had been one of the residences of Prince-Archbishop Clemens August of Bavaria.[1] With its network of canals and moats, its great central building—white, gabled, and flanked by corner towers—Heimerzheim stood on an island reached by a succession of bridges, like a summer palace in ancient China. Its immense grounds were left in a half-wild state where deer peacefully grazed and the familiar mixture of mystery and nature on the doorstep made Heimerzheim seem to us like a fairy-tale castle. Nothing was easier there than to retreat into a secret world. Imagination and children's games could hardly have found a more propitious place to develop.

We had a liberal upbringing at Heimerzheim, something that always surprised the guests who passed through—and they were many, since our mother believed that those who had the good fortune to live in a great residence should keep an open house. But for all that, our upbringing was not permissive. Life was very clearly structured, framed by a few strictly defined moral principles: for example, it was forbidden to torture animals. Within this framework, we enjoyed a great deal of latitude.

My father, Albert von Boeselager, was a cultured man of letters. His mother's side of the family hailed from Brussels, and he considered the European nobility a unitary body. He hunted all over the Continent and spoke four or five languages.

Because of this, he attached particular importance to learning how to make proper use of freedom—and the capacity for Christian discernment that was for him its corollary—and also to hunting. Georg received his first rifle as a Christmas present in 1928, when he was only thirteen years old. At fifteen, my brother's list of kills already included some 150 head of game. His passion was such that he managed to sneak a disassembled rifle into our boarding school in Bad Godesberg—with my complicity, I must admit. When the housemaster Father Strasser made the rounds of the bedrooms to check the students' bags, we were forced once again to engage in a ruse. Each of us slipped part of the rifle into his shorts—Georg the barrel and I the stock—while the inspection took place. The maneuver was acrobatic, because it was strictly forbidden to put our hands in our pockets, but we somehow had to prevent the parts of the rifle from slipping out.

It was hunting that truly shaped our behavior in nature, and profoundly influenced our way of life. Georg, in particular, learned to find his way in the forest even before the sun came up; to creep up to within a few meters of a woodcock without scaring the bird away; to slip through the bushes without making the leaves rustle so as not to frighten the deer; to disappear into the vegetation, perfectly camouflaged; to wait patiently, silent and inactive; and to act at the right fraction of a second. In a word, hunting, practiced in a group or in the course of long solitary hikes, with that passion for animals that marks true nature lovers, made Georg a real Indian. He remained one. He was later to find this training extremely valuable.

Hunting was not only a way of hardening the body. It prepared us, without our being aware of it, for the laws of life, for the struggles of existence: saving one's strength, fleeing from an adversary, recovering, knowing how to use cunning, adapting to the enemy, assessing risk. We learned how to keep our sangfroid in the tumult of dogs excited by the battle, how to cut the throat of a stag or a boar in the coup de grâce and look without revulsion at the dark red fluid bubbling out of mortal wounds. We did not shiver upon seeing the brown trickle running down the pale pelt of a young deer, or the bloody foam staining the chops of an animal exhausted by the chase. We withstood the glassy stare of the dead animal and, finally, collected these bloody, damp trophies, the *spolia opima* of modern times. Hunting also accustomed us to the laws of violent death, internalized the notion of an offering. Yes, hunting was a preparation for the supreme sacrifice—the sacrifice of life.

The education we received at Godesberg did not differ from what we were taught at Heimerzheim, which I would call relaxed Catholicism. My family was profoundly Catholic, with a centuries-old history linked to that of the German Catholic princes. In the seventeenth century, our ancestors, the Heyden-Belderbusches, from whom we had inherited the Heimerzheim castle, had been ministers of the powerful archbishop of Cologne. During the same period, the Satzenhovens, from whom we had inherited the Kreuzberg estate, had served the prince electors of Mainz.

As children, Georg and I were very close. Only two years apart, we were like Castor and Pollux—natural playmates, and accomplices in the same practical jokes. But this intimacy, which made us almost a separate unit among our siblings, did not prevent us from developing different qualities; nor did it diminish the natural ascen-

Philipp and his siblings in front of the family house:
he is the fifth from the left, in front of Georg.

dancy of the elder child over the younger. As a duo, we complemented each other. Georg was physically more robust, more athletic, more intuitive, and instinctively perceptive regarding people, situations, and things. I, on the other hand, was more reflective and analytical. Two anecdotes from our early childhood clearly show our difference in character.

At Heimerzheim, the grounds were full of wild deer. The animals sometimes came quite close to the house. One day, our older brothers Antonius and Hermann, who were then not quite ten, were amusing themselves by throwing pebbles at one of the deer, trying to provoke it. Sitting behind a stone bench, Georg was watching carefully. The roebuck, suddenly responding to the little devils' challenge, was about to attack. Georg reacted with lightning speed; all of five years old, he seized the rifle that Antonius had left leaning against the bench and shot at the animal. *Ka-boom!* Bowled over by the rifle's recoil, Georg fell backward. Fortunately, he was not injured. But the explosion had frightened away the roebuck.

As for me, when I was four years old I distinguished myself at a family dinner. Our cousin zu Stolberg-Stolberg had been seriously wounded in the head during the Great War. The surgeons had installed a silver plate on his skull to close the hole left by enemy fire, and he lived until the 1960s. I had heard about this extraordinary operation and wanted to see the result for myself. Climbing silently onto a chair, I leaned over my cousin's head and

Philipp, nine years old, with his father's hunting trophy,
September 1926.

began to examine, discreetly and carefully, the bald area where the precious metal shone. They say that I then cried, disappointed, "That's not silver! There's no hallmark!" As a reward for this impertinent observation, I received a couple of slaps.

To tell the truth, our father never took much interest in his children's scholastic progress. After several years of taking lessons at home, however, the boys had to be subjected to modern education. "School," our father said, sighing, "is an obligation these days. It's very boring, but you've got to do it!" So we were enrolled in the Aloïsius Jesuit secondary school in Godesberg, on the outskirts of Bonn. As it turned out, entering boarding school was not very traumatic. Heimerzheim was then less than an hour's drive from the school. The Jesuit curriculum at Aloïsius did not seek to train priests, but to reconcile the sacred and the profane in human beings, and to keep alive the flame of faith amid the chaos of the world. The practice of religion was not supposed to be an end in itself; it was intended to slip naturally into the schedules, the lives, and, as it were, the skins of the young boys. The five or six years we spent in Godesberg helped root in us a solid, authentic, uncomplicated, moderate faith. Ultimately, we acquired more a way of behaving than a body of knowledge, although nothing was omitted from the regular curriculum. In any case, we learned the most important thing that can be taught: how to learn.

The headmaster of the boarding school was a patriot.

As he saw it, the Christian values, humanism, sense of honor, respect for others, and tradition of intellectual rigor and critical vigilance that had long characterized Jesuit pedagogy were not incompatible with patriotism. Interestingly, none of my classmates later became a Nazi supporter. This fact, which was rather exceptional in my generation, deserves to be noted.

2

The Time of Choices

1933–36

In 1933, when the Nazis came to power, Georg was not yet seventeen years old; I was only fifteen. This event, although it later turned out to be crucial for us and our families, left us rather indifferent at the time. Our parents, though they certainly did not adhere to the ideology of the Nazi Party, were not sorry to see the end of the Weimar Republic.

We knew what it was to feel humiliated after a defeat. Because we lived on the west bank of the Rhine, which was under Allied occupation between 1919 and 1926, we saw Canadian, British, and then French troops—chiefly drawn from the colonies—march past. These years of peacetime occupation were long and burdensome. For Germans, the situation was incomprehensible: enemy troops had not entered the country on the western frontier and there had been no invasion during the war, but it was the Treaty of Versailles, considered unjust and designed to ruin the country, that had brought about foreign occupation. An occupation, even a tranquil one, is hardly likely to strengthen friendship among peoples. But the occupation of the Ruhr from 1923 to 1926 was accompanied by violence and turmoil, and resulted in 121 summary executions and tens of thousands of expulsions. It also led to a general strike, instigated by Chancellor Cuno, and the economic collapse of the industrial heart of Germany, which caused terrifying inflation. All that, I think, accentuated the Rhinelanders' already very strong prejudice against the French, who had been seen for centuries as troublesome neighbors. The humiliations inflicted by the occupying forces did not escape my notice when I was a child. I remember that my parents were forbidden to attend my grandmother's funeral, on the pretext that my father was a reserve officer. I also recall how we congratulated Father Seelen, who had dared to sing the German national anthem, which was strictly prohibited on the west bank, in full view of the French troops. Fortunately Father Seelen was a Dutch citizen, and the French could not arrest him. That is how, as young men, we practiced as much resistance as possible.

My father believed in European unity before it became fashionable; he was not at all inclined to vindictiveness. But as a former officer in the Great War, he was a patriot, and he wanted to see Germany regain all its rights as a great nation. He communicated this desire to us without imposing it on us. And our elder brother Antonius quite naturally joined the paramilitary organization Stahlhelm.

I can understand if a foreign reader mistrusts German patriots' political position in that period, and is tempted to see in it an unacceptable compromise with the goals pursued by Adolf Hitler. However, we German patriots were nonetheless able to tell the difference. We had no more cause to be ashamed of wanting to restore Germany than had the French, who, in 1914, wanted to restore Alsace and Lorraine to France.

I must describe something that happened to me at that time that taught me a little about the methods of Hitler's men. In 1934 the chancellor of the Reich came to Bonn. Curious, I climbed over my boarding school's wall, accompanied by a classmate. We approached the Dreesen Hotel, where the chancellor was supposed to be staying, and found a hiding place where we might at least catch a glimpse of him on the steps. We were found out. Two SS men picked us up and, without further investigation, simply locked us in a garage. We were terrified that the headmaster of the school, informed of our escape, might punish us. Our internment, without food and without sleep, lasted until the early hours of the morning, but once the chancellor had departed, we were set free. Miraculously, our desertion had not been noticed at school. During that day and the following night we had plenty to think about.

The somewhat suspicious nature of the Nazi movement was soon revealed in another way. The headmaster of our school in Bad Godesberg, Father Rodewyck, a Jesuit and a former military officer in the Great War, was not indifferent to the revival of patriotism. But he was able to channel the ardor of the boys entrusted to him by providing a Christian framework within his school and avoiding any pollution by Nazi ideology. Thus in 1933 Georg founded a Catholic patriotic movement in the school whose scouting spirit was indicated by its attachment to moral and religious values. It was called the Jungstahlhelm. Along similar lines, the Jesuit school founded a movement on the model of Hitler's Deutsche Jungvolk or Pimpfen, whose activities (camping, hiking, and the like) then seemed quite innocent. Father Rodewyck had seen the risk that hearts and souls might be won by the Nazi Party's youth organizations, and he preferred to infiltrate the movement using boys like us. Our principal thought he had done what was necessary to keep control of the organization. But it gradually escaped his grasp and that of the school.

It was at this time that another important episode occurred. I belonged to a club devoted to Our Lady: the Congregation of Mary. One fine day in the summer of 1937, the head of my group of Pimpfen, a nice fellow, came to tell me that belonging to the valiant Pimpfen was incompatible with religion, and so I had to choose between the two. I was intelligent; he was sure that he would succeed in persuading me to give up my membership in the Congregation of Mary without hesitation. But I flatly refused. I found it intolerable to be forced to make such a choice, and did not hesitate. I have to admit that I did not reveal the precise motive for my refusal. I told him only that preparing for my final school examination prevented me from continuing to participate in Pimpfen activities. The pretext seemed valid, and it was accepted.

Georg took his final exam in the summer of 1934. He had already made a decision regarding his future: he wanted to be a military officer. My brother had a taste for action and initiative. He excelled in all athletic disciplines, had inexhaustible energy, and showed great endurance. He liked the outdoor life. And in the end, he was interested in human psychology. Objectively, everything pointed him toward this profession. At that time people believed, not without a certain naïveté, that entering the army was a way of serving one's country without serving the government. It seemed to us that the army was the only institution that had remained faithful to its principles and was capable, through its vitality and culture, of preserving its identity and, especially, its autonomy. In 1934, for a young man like Georg, a military career still seemed to make it possible to reconcile a taste for action with independence.

Georg then had to choose his branch. He opted for the cavalry. He was built like a jockey; when he asked to be admitted to the regiment, he was told that he was not heavy enough. My father wrote to the commandant and appealed to the ministry. Finally, the military administration agreed that except on this one point, Georg had all of the required physical aptitudes. They were not wrong. During his years of training in military schools and then in the Paderborn Fifteenth Cavalry Regiment, Georg spent a great deal of time perfecting his equestrian technique, and much of his leisure time competing in races. By 1939 he had participated in about a hundred competitions.

In 1936 I was confronted by the same choice. I was attracted to a diplomatic career; to that end, I had even begun learning Arabic. I could already write its alphabet and read a little. Shortly after taking my examination, I went to ask the advice of my maternal grandfather, Baron von Salis-Soglio, a liberal man with firm convictions. In his youth, he had distinguished himself by resigning his post as a government official in protest against a disciplinary transfer to East Prussia, which he had received as punishment for participating in a Corpus Christi procession. To do this in a part of Germany that was historically Catholic, and had been joined to Protestant Prussia after the treaties of Vienna, was proof of a strongly independent spirit. We had full confidence in his judgments. My grandfather told me straight out, "My boy, in diplomacy, it's not always good to tell the whole truth; but with Nazis, you'd have to simply lie. No, that wouldn't be suitable for you! Choose the army instead; war is coming."

This advice was typical of my grandfather's lucidity: Germany had just rearmed, despite the provisions of the Versailles Treaty, and in March 1936 it had remilitarized the west bank of the Rhine: the smell of gunpowder was in the air. It was judicious to learn the soldier's trade. So after having completed my classes in Döberitz during the summer of 1938, I joined my brother in the Paderborn Cavalry Regiment. At first, I was in the reserves. Then, following Georg's example, I began training for active duty as an officer.

In the meantime, I had done my compulsory national service in Merseburg. My group was made up of fifteen Rhinelanders and the same number of Bavarians, and the two contingents were unable to speak with each other because each knew only its own dialect. We were supposed to help construct a dike. I was an engine driver, and my job was to bring construction materials to the site. The atmosphere wasn't bad; we had agreed not to compete with each other, and the Bavarians conscientiously soaped the rails before dawn so that the materials would arrive more slowly. Everybody benefited. But it was a spartan life. We slept on pallets on the concrete floor of a shed. The people in charge were not intelligent. The indoctrination sessions were so mediocre that they frequently ended a quarter of an hour early in a gale of laughter. I was careful not to judge this experience negatively; this obligation was additional proof of the absurdity of certain of the regime's measures, but after all, I had taken advantage of it to harden myself a little, and I got along well with my fellow Rhinelanders.

It would be an exaggeration to say that our vigilance toward the regime had already been awakened at that point. The officers were trained in a completely apolitical way, as if the Wehrmacht, the heir of the Reichswehr and an eternal institution, were situated sufficiently above the vicissitudes of the time to be indifferent to them. We were entirely devoted to our military training and, since we lived in barracks far from the cities and were cut off from the press, we were not well informed. I have to admit that the famous encyclical *Mit brennender Sorge* (*With Burning Anxiety*), which denounced Nazism, had hardly any effect on me. I was barely twenty years old; at that age, one easily forgets encyclicals read from the pulpit, and one certainly does not read them for amusement!

However, one important point attracted my attention. For a time after Hitler's accession to power, my father had a Nazi Party card. This was not because of personal conviction, or even opportunism. He had allowed himself to be persuaded by people from the village who had come in 1934 to ask him to join the party. Our father was a principal figure in the Rhineland's nobility. I think he saw the question in the following terms, as did many other people of his social cohort: Did he have the right, on the pretext of belonging to the aristocracy, to disdain this vast movement of national renewal? Did he have the privilege of not joining in this groundswell that was carrying millions of Germans in its wake? Did he, whom the local population considered a true gentleman, have good reasons for preserving a detachment that might look like arrogance or folly, or even scorn for the popular elements that constituted most of the movement's membership?

These concerns notwithstanding, our father quickly returned to his feelings of reservation and even outright hostility concerning the regime. In 1937 the government, which was violating with increasing frequency the concordat signed with the Holy See in July 1933, decided to remove crucifixes from the schools. This attack, even if only symbolic, on Germany's Christian identity seemed unacceptable to him. Since 1919, the Weimar Republic had been trying to find, region by region, a delicate balance in the relations between church and state.[1] More generally, the church's discreet influence persisted at all levels in young people's education. The Nazis' sabotage threatened to destroy all these achievements. Moreover, it said a great deal about the regime's totalitarian aims. Therefore, our father resigned from the party in 1938, at a time when the annexation of Austria was leading many people to join it. The Nazis responded by forcing him to resign from organizations of which he was the president, notably the National League for the Defense of Hunting.

Another ground for concern was the regime's anti-Jewish policy. From legal restrictions, which had rapidly become so numerous that it was difficult to tell which ones were marginal and which were essential, it progressed to physical intimidation, and finally to routine violence. There were three Jewish families in our little town of Heimerzheim. Our father, seeing the danger, advised them to flee the country. He even offered to pay their travel expenses. Two of the families followed his advice and emigrated to the United States. The father in the third family, whose name was Moses, elected not to go. He thought the Iron Cross he had been awarded for service in the trenches in 1914 would ensure his safety. He was sadly mistaken. A few years later, he was arrested along with the rest of his family. We never saw them again.

Even if the information available in the barracks was limited, Kristallnacht, in November 1938, did not escape our attention. I remember that it was talked about quite freely among officers and students. In the local newspaper, we read only that "three shops were ransacked on Westendstrasse." At first, we did not realize that this was part of a more general phenomenon that was affecting all of Germany. Further information dribbled in over the next few days, especially through correspondence between our men and their families in different parts of the country. For us, public order was nonnegotiable, and a pogrom was an unprecedented violation of rights and public peace, inadmissible in a civilized country. We all agreed—perhaps with a certain naïveté—that if we had been present in town when exactions were being made, we would have cited the criminal code regarding legitimate self-defense. Our commandant assured us that the courts would take action. Later on, when we realized the full measure of the atrocities, we were for a time persuaded that the generals would act. For us, it was unthinkable that the law could be violated with impunity in Germany, without anyone doing anything about it. But nothing was done, apart from our commandant's assurances and consolations.

The cavalry regiment was hermetically sealed off from much of the outside world. Constructing a spirit of comradeship was more important for us than pretending to be citizens of the world. Sports were far more important than political discussion. Jumping and dressage were our daily occupations. Having fewer physical abilities than Georg, I had to catch up. To lose weight and so as not to receive humiliating scores on the racecourse, I even had to fast from Tuesday to Saturday. A hard school! But a good one, for my captain was Rudolf Lippert, the Olympic equestrian champion at the 1936 games.

The days were long and the training was vigorous and encouraging. Each morning, summer and winter, we left on our motorcycles at dawn and headed for Quelle, forty-eight kilometers away, near Bielefeld, where there was a fine racecourse. The regiment kept racehorses

Berlin, September 1938: parade of the Paderborn Fifteenth Cavalry Regiment honoring Mussolini. Georg leads the detachment; Philipp is the last on the right in the first row.

there, which were made available to officers in order to improve our skills. The horses would be waiting for us, already saddled up. We would leap into the saddle, make two or three circuits around the course, then hand the reins to a groom and hop back on our motorcycles to hurry back to school and shower. Our orderlies were waiting for us with towels and fresh clothes. Then we reported, more or less in good spirits, for the morning roll call, and by seven-thirty we were ready to begin the workday proper, which included several more hours of equestrian exercise.

3

The Phony War

1939–40

When war broke out on September 1, 1939, the Paderborn Cavalry Regiment—which was for us almost a second family—was dissolved, like the thirteen other units of mounted cavalry in the Wehrmacht before mobilization. We were divided up into fifty-two squadrons scattered over thirty-three infantry divisions. We were supposed to be integrated into reconnaissance battalions whose mission was—by reconnoitering, establishing bridgeheads, and, in short, performing all kinds of bold actions—to prepare the way for the less-mobile units of heavy infantry. The reconnaissance battalions, each consisting of about a thousand men, included a staff to handle support functions (administration, food supplies, intelligence), a cavalry squadron, a cycle squadron, and a heavy motorized squadron. The battalions had excellent communications equipment, especially radios.

The first months of the war passed rather peacefully. Georg and I were assigned to the area along the borders with Luxembourg and France, Georg in the Sixth Infantry Division, and I in the Eighty-sixth. Georg became head of the Sixth Cavalry Squadron, with our elder brother Tonio, who was a reservist, under his command. Tonio in turn headed a detachment of about fifty cavalrymen. To tell the truth, this "phony war" was not without fighting, even on a front that was said to be quiet. On September 8, no less than six divisions of the French Fourth Army advanced several kilometers into German territory, between Forbach and Bitche, and were about to enter into contact with the Siegfried Line, which was situated at some distance from the border. Georg's unit was involved in a few skirmishes with the French troops. As for me, I was assigned to retake a French position in the middle of the night. The enemy's disarray was complete, because they hadn't anticipated that we would approach it by the most difficult side. The French withdrew from our sector in October.

This period of semi-inactivity allowed the officers to complete the training of the reservists who had been mobilized during the summer and—a temptation not to be resisted when autumn came—to hunt in the game-filled forests along the banks of the Moselle.

4

A Dive for Victory

JUNE 9, 1940

Incorporated into the Fourth Army, part of Army Group B, the Sixth Infantry Division entered France on May 16, a few days after the large armored and motorized groups that had overwhelmed the French defenses. By May 28, it had reached the Somme and was beginning to tack toward the southwest. Paris was caught in a sling on the north and west, while Army Group A, crossing the Aisne, threatened the capital's eastern flank and then headed for Burgundy. On June 9, the Sixth Division forced its way across the Seine and set up bridgeheads around Les Andelys.[1] At noon, the French blew up the bridge at Les Andelys, which a German advance unit had tried to seize. For the Germans, the day had begun in confusion; the Sixth Reconnaissance Battalion moved a few kilometers up the Seine, but toward three o'clock in the afternoon, the French blew up the bridge at Courcelles.

It was then that Georg's sense of initiative came fully to the fore. He had noticed an organizational weakness in the French defenses. Opposite the hamlet of Les Mousseaux, there were only a few isolated troops, and they lacked heavy artillery. At that place, the river narrowed slightly and was only about 180 meters across. The banks of the river were muddy, spongy, unstable, and covered with tall grass, reeds, and even brambles—no place to go swimming! But Georg quickly made a decision. It was pointless to wait for inflatable boats; precious minutes would be lost. He selected a group of good swimmers. Led by my brother, twelve men rapidly undressed and moved into the river, armed with a few rifles and hand grenades. The rest of the unit was assigned to provide cover for their attack. Three of these men drowned almost at once, probably as a result of the shock of the cold water and exhaustion after almost four weeks of constant activity. In addition, for the past two days, the squadron had been without food supplies.

The French were taken completely by surprise. They could not have anticipated an attack by a small group of cavalry that had made itself amphibious. Georg's little squad had caught its breath on a tiny island in the middle of the river. A few French snipers were hidden in the vegetation on the opposite bank, but the fire from a German machine gun set up on the east bank quickly dislodged them from their hiding place. The west bank of the Seine was now undefended. Georg and his men rapidly occupied it, and climbed a few meters up the embankment. They had to stop when they reached the top. The village of Grandvillers, which lay in front of them, still had a few defenders, and it would have been madness to operate in the open. The alert had no doubt been sounded, and French reinforcements would be on their way. But the little group had established a bridgehead. Inflatable boats were now bringing men and matériel from the other side of the river. In a few minutes, sixty men and some light artillery had been unloaded on the west bank. An hour later, the whole cavalry squadron, both men and horses, had passed over.

Shortly afterward, a detachment led by our brother Tonio took Grand-Villiers. Georg and his men stopped a French motorized column dead in its tracks as it advanced along the road to Les Andelys. Twenty minutes later, they intercepted an artillery column. During the fifteen hours that followed, the French made four attempts to retake Grand-Villiers, all in vain.

Even if, on June 9, the victory was already won, Georg's exploit nonetheless entered the annals of the Wehrmacht and made my brother famous for a few days. It was, in a way, another version of the seizure of Sedan on May 10. Crossing the Seine made it possible to attack

Paris from the opposite side and to deprive our enemies of any hope of turning the military situation around—if they still entertained such hopes.

On June 16 Georg and his men distinguished themselves once again. The scene took place at Marchainville, near the castle of Persay. The French were defending themselves well. An artillery battalion prevented the Germans from advancing. Georg and his squad managed to get around the obstacle, and they abruptly attacked from the rear. There were no casualties on either side; the French immediately surrendered. The booty was invaluable: three 75 mm guns, gun carriages, and . . . the prospect of a good dinner. To the amazement of the French, Georg collected all the provisions and canned goods, and decided "fifty-fifty" with an eloquent gesture. The French and the Germans thus ate their meals side by side. They almost managed to make friends during this improvised picnic. But then my brother suddenly noticed several French tanks approaching: the power relationship had been reversed. It was no longer time for joking. In a few seconds, Georg and his men packed up, left their dining companions and the food, and got out of the clearing as fast as they could. My brother's military tactics and behavior inclined him to avoid unnecessary fighting and to save lives.

5

A Promise

While Georg was leading his men through the Paris basin, I was serving as aide-de-camp to the commandant of the 186th Reconnaissance Battalion, within the 86th Infantry Division of Army Group A. We had started out from Hermeskeil, near Trier, traversed Luxembourg, and entered France by way of Sedan. After hard fighting near Rethel, we were getting ready to move on to the Langres Plateau, making a wide sweep toward the Swiss border.[1]

On June 17, my battalion was stationed in Allainville, near Grand. In the commandant's absence, I was temporarily in charge. We were supposed to attack the town of Prez, a few kilometers to the south, when a certain incident prevented us from doing so. The head of a heavy artillery battery, a man named Auer who was very concerned about his own comfort, had brought along his personal car, and this was equipped with a radio (something unusual at the time). It was late in the afternoon when he came to tell me what he'd just heard: a French news program had announced that Marshal Pétain was preparing to ask Germany for an armistice. I mentioned this to Rudolf von Gersdorff, head of the operations section of the division's staff. The news was not official; there was neither a confirmed cease-fire nor any formal order in this regard. But we believed that the information was crucial and justified our change of conduct. It seemed clear that it would be useless and even criminal to shed any more blood at this stage. Therefore, on our own initiative—and this was certainly not usual for officers of a victorious army—we decided to establish contact with the enemy.

A French colonel who had been taken prisoner told us where the road had been mined. After attaching a white flag to a broomstick, we requisitioned a bugle and a car, and in this noble equipage Gersdorff and I approached the French lines. A sentry came to inquire what we wanted. The officer in charge of the French battalion was sought out. He was a mere lieutenant; like me, he was standing in for the leader of the battalion, who had left the day before to get instructions. The French lieutenant, after having us blindfolded, took us to the battalion's command post. It was 5:00 p.m. The Frenchman knew nothing about the request for a cease-fire and stated that he had been instructed to hold his position until precisely 7:00 p.m. Afterward, he was supposed to withdraw. As gentlemen, we thus agreed that the Germans would start moving after 7:00 p.m., and would occupy the village only after the last French troops had left it.

Satisfied with this arrangement, we returned to Allainville. Gersdorff asked me to see to the execution of the terms of the agreement, and went back to the divisional headquarters, which he had left several hours earlier and to which he said he absolutely must return.

A few moments later, Lieutenant Colonel Doege came up to me. The infantry regiment he commanded was moving south, and he coldly informed me of his intention to attack Prez.

"Impossible, Colonel," I replied. "We have an agreement with the French. They've asked for a cease-fire." I explained the situation. The lieutenant colonel didn't want to hear about it, either because he wished to distinguish himself by some new feat, or because he didn't have much confidence in what I said.

"Sorry to displease you," he said, "but I'm going to give the order to attack."

I could see that he was determined, and that his foolishness was probably going to cost dozens of lives in both camps. I decided to pull out all the stops. As calmly as possible, and fully aware of the disciplinary consequences that might result, I drew my pistol and pointed it at the colonel.

"It is I who am sorry, but if you give this order I will have to shoot you," I said, very carefully.

The lieutenant colonel exploded with anger. But seeing the pistol pointed at him, and seeing that I looked as though I was actually prepared to shoot him, he yielded. The French battalion was saved. Everything went as planned, without drop of blood being shed. Few people knew what had happened, and we tried to keep it quiet. But we were unable to keep the news from circulating among the staffs. The story became almost a legend—in some versions, I actually fired. Fortunately, as the anecdote spread and became distorted, the names of the two people involved were forgotten. In any case, until the end of the war Doege and I took care to avoid each other.

6

A Lightning Campaign

JUNE–NOVEMBER 1941

The end of the campaign in France inaugurated a peaceful time of almost nine months. We took advantage of this relative calm to train men and horses, and especially to hunt. Fate had been good to me: I was based south of Orléans, in the middle of Sologne, a hunter's paradise. There I lived in a house deserted by wealthy Parisians who had fled to the South. I still have very pleasant memories of those few months when the German occupation was, obviously, still not too painful for the French, or at least did not yet elicit hostile reactions.

My brother Georg was less fortunate. During the summer his squadron was located in Chauny, on the road from Poitiers to Angoulême. Chauny was almost in the South, in that part of Vienne close to the Charente. The sparsely wooded countryside, rather poorly maintained, was hardly suitable for hunting, and poachers seemed already to have skimmed off the area's limited supply of game: there remained neither big game, nor tracking, nor even battues; there were no wild ducks or partridges. Cats (which Georg abhorred), dogs, and sparrows were the only wild animals to be found. No matter! On July 23, a few days after they had established themselves in Chauny, Georg organized his first hunt and invited the head of the battalion.

Georg's superior was cantoned some fifteen kilometers away, and the division was scattered over the whole department of Vienne. Lodged in a mansion that looked out on the main square, my brother reigned over his village and commanded his 250 men as he wished. They were, however, not entirely idle; during the summer, his squadron had to deal with the flow of tens of thousands of French who had headed south with the exodus, and were now slowly returning north along National Highway 10. The long line of automobiles loaded with mattresses, bicycles, cooking utensils, and packages of various kinds stretched as far as one could see, and the heat was merciless—as high as 50°C (122°F) in the sun. In addition, Georg and his men had to cope with the angry outbursts of an exasperated population. But it was not yet time for revolt. The French still didn't feel that sensation of being crushed that would lead them to realize that they had been completely and lastingly defeated.

They did not yet bend under the weight of the foreign occupation. The infernal cycle of acts of resistance and repressions, and especially the cycle of persecutions and deportations, had not yet begun. A feeling of indifference was pervasive. One had to get along, and customs inspired by mutual tolerance were quickly established.[1]

Georg's stay in Vienne was soon over. His division was called upon to participate in the top-secret preparations for the invasion of England. In September 1940, it started moving toward the English Channel. The soldiers took up their position within the Cotentin, the Calvados, and the Orne. Georg was very active in training his men.

But it was not toward England that the Sixth Infantry Division was finally to direct its forces. Despite intense bombardments and peace offers followed by threats, Britain, isolated and bled dry, did not falter. Above all, it did not give up hope of victory. So in March 1941, the Sixth Infantry Division was transferred to the far reaches of East Prussia and Poland, very near the USSR's border. No information regarding the high command's intentions filtered down. However, even the less lucid among us noticed the growing concentration of troops, the acceleration of training, and the energy expended by the battalion's new commandant, Major Hirsch, on exploring the border area. All this was merely the prelude to an invasion of the Soviet Union. The attack began in the early hours of June 22, 1941. The Eighty-sixth Infantry

Division, in which I was an officer, was brought in from France only a few weeks later. We were thus less exposed to the first clashes with the enemy.

At the beginning of a battle, the role of a reconnaissance battalion was crucial. Reconnoitering the terrain, making raids to take prisoners or equipment (munitions and maps), harassing the enemy to demoralize him without investing great human resources, dislodging hidden snipers, making sure that columns advancing at very different speeds joined up where they were supposed to: such were, in their diversity, the scouts' missions. On May 18, in preparation for the offensive, the command of the Ninth Army decided to split the elite unit constituted by the Sixth Reconnaissance Battalion into two parts. The first, called the advance battalion, still under Hirsch's orders, was placed directly under the command of the Ninth Army. Georg, who was about to be promoted to the rank of captain, was given the leadership of a reconnaissance battalion that consisted only of a cavalry squadron and a cycle squadron, reinforced by an intelligence detachment, and especially by a mortar battery, a heavy machine gun, and an antiaircraft battery. The battalion played a very active role in the first hours of the offensive. By the evening of June 22, Georg's forces had reached their objective. They were asked to establish a bridgehead on the Memel River. After crossing ten kilometers of marshes and forests, Georg encountered stiff resistance from the enemy. On June 25, the reconnaissance forces were joined together again, but during this short interval the mounted cavalry, used for the first time in a relatively isolated manner, had shown its flexibility in all sorts of situations.

Around the middle of July, it was again the reconnaissance work carried out by Georg's men that allowed the Sixth Division to take, almost without losses, the citadel of Polozk on the Dvina. On July 27, barely a month after the offensive had started, the Sixth Battalion had covered a thousand kilometers by forced march. The exhausted infantrymen's feet were bleeding, despite the efforts of the physicians, who distributed large quantities of talcum powder and ointment. The vehicles were dented and covered with dust; logs were being used as bumpers. They advanced laboriously on rutted dirt roads and sank up to their axles on sandy tracks. Their oil pans scraped the ground, their engines coughed, sputtered, spat out oil, and left a trail of nuts and bolts. And when, by some miracle, the convoys were able to get up some speed on solid roads, each vehicle raised a long cloud of dust that spread over a hundred meters, enveloping those behind it. The horses moved forward almost imperturbably, caring little about the marshes or the dust so long as the cavalry detachments were separated from each other by at least a hundred meters. They went briskly around obstacles, plunged up to their chests in the sticky water of the marshes, galloped . . . and always arrived at the rendezvous on time. But the cavalry couldn't advance alone.

It was mobile, but not invulnerable. The strikes it attempted resulted in casualties every time its troops were not properly covered by the artillery.

Until late July, the advance of the units to which Georg and I belonged was extremely rapid. We were on the road to Moscow, taking Napoléon's route, more or less. The enemy's resistance was weak, and his morale was failing. In view of the collapse of the Russian army, which was, moreover, practicing scorched-earth tactics, opinion in the Soviet Union was on the whole very favorable toward us.[2] So we were optimistic about the outcome of the operations. We thought Russia's fate would be decided within six weeks. But Russia wasn't France. A blitzkrieg was impossible in a country of several tens of millions of square kilometers. At the end of July, our advance halted. On this terrain, the enemy had recovered. The threat to Moscow was too direct not to elicit a response, and the Sixth Infantry Division had to adopt a defensive position around Borki on the Mesha.

The month of August was difficult. There were daily skirmishes with the enemy. Placed under the authority of the Fifty-eighth Infantry Regiment, Georg's unit was being used for reconnaissance missions on the left flank, which the Russians had penetrated by crossing the Dvina. On August 1, the cavalry repelled an enemy battalion, which outnumbered them four to one, back onto the far bank of the river. On August 2, the reconnaissance battalion found itself surrounded after a coordinated attack by two Russian cavalry divisions. My brother's squadron was quickly brought back to the battalion to which it was attached. There was no time to lose. Although it was seven p.m. and getting dark, Georg surprised the attacking forces by striking their southern flank, between Agejeva and Shichova. Supported by artillery, he inflicted severe losses on the adversary. The fighting went on all night and the following day. The day after that, the Russian attack was over, and the connection between the division and its reconnaissance battalion was restored.

However, these missions soon took a tragic turn. On the evening of August 4, Tonio, who had been put under Georg's direct command in one of the skirmishes in which the squadron was regularly engaged, was hit by a bullet and fell from his mount. He remained on the battlefield while Georg and his cavalrymen, carried forward by their momentum, pursued the scattered Russians. The medics ran to help Tonio and discovered that he had a wound in his abdomen—a serious one, according to a preliminary diagnosis carried out in the twilight, but not mortal. His intestines and spleen had been damaged. He was taken to the field hospital, but died the next day from an embolism after an operation that seemed to have gone well. He was buried in a nearby cemetery, near an old church that the Soviets had converted into a wheat barn. Georg and I were shattered. Fortunately, we were able to see each other on August 26 and 27, because my division was in a neighboring sector. These moments spent together provided us with a little consolation and a way to share our suffering as brothers. This was, alas, not the only sacrifice that year was to impose on us, because on November 30 we would lose our youngest brother as well.

In early October we began offensive operations again. Georg's division moved forward into a marshy area that was impracticable for motorized vehicles. The autumn, which was warm, hampered the armies' advance: the freeze was late in coming. It rained constantly, obstinately. The roads turned into sewers. Trucks, bogged down in the mud, ran out of fuel, and food supplies could not get through. At times Georg and his horses were almost a hundred kilometers ahead of the rest of their division. The month of October practically decided the fate of the war. It was soon clear that we could not take Moscow before December, when the terrible Russian winter would set in. The officers thought about the ill-fated French episode in 1812. The autumn had stalled our forward momentum, and winter would prevent any further advance.

In any case, the Sixth Infantry succeeded in fulfilling its assignment. At the end of October, it descended the Volga, passed to the north of the capital, and reached Kalinin (now the city of Tver). Georg and his men crossed over to the east bank of the Volga in a sector infested with enemies. They pushed as far as the Tma, one of the great river's tributaries. In a few hours, without losing a single man or being observed, they explored dozens of square kilometers, wrote reports, and sent to their headquarters all the information that might be useful for a prospective penetration. By November 15, they had an impressive record in the field: they had covered more than 1,300 kilometers, and taken prizes that were considerable for a unit of 200 men: 700 prisoners, 175 horses, 60 horse-drawn vehicles, 10 trucks, and a tank! This record was transmitted with get-well wishes to all the squadron's wounded, who were scattered in various military hospitals.

The campaign had been just as brilliant for the division to which I belonged. As far as Smolensk, our losses had been minimal. The fighting around Smolensk lasted from July 10 to September 10. About three hundred thousand Soviet troops and three thousand tanks were surrounded; the Soviets were not about to get themselves killed for Joseph Stalin. We gave them back their churches, which had been closed or transformed into storage buildings years earlier. The sinister Commissar Order, which called for the execution of Soviet political commissars who had been taken prisoner, never reached my unit and was not applied in my area: under these conditions, whole battalions of Russians were surrendering without a fight. One day, I sent Second Lieutenant Nagel on patrol a little to the east of Vilnius, and he came back in the evening with about two thousand prisoners. They were still fully equipped, because the fifteen men in

Nagel's detachment were not numerous enough to dis-
arm them. His men were riding alongside the prisoners
like shepherds amid a peaceful flock. It was an incredible
sight, unparalleled so far as I know in recent military
history.

A few weeks after the fighting ended around Smolensk, the general in command of the division ordered me
to scout out the possibilities for crossing the Volga at a
ford. Because of the mud, horse-drawn vehicles could not
be used, and all the motor vehicles had prudently been
taken back to the main road to Moscow. Only horsemen
could reconnoiter the area ahead. We started out toward
Kalinin with provisions for a few days. Using a compass,
and guided by the information provided by scouts, we
rode for four or five hours and then stopped in a village to
bake bread in a farm, surrounded by Russians, because
the field canteen had remained with the vehicles. The
days went by without any contact with our division. It
was as if we had suddenly been transported to the age of
the Thirty Years' War. Our squadron encountered neither Russian nor German soldiers. When we arrived in
Kalinin, the Volga was completely frozen over, and our
search for a ford was no longer relevant. Moreover,
armored divisions had just taken up positions nearby.

Three days later, the division's chaplains arrived in
Kalinin. Like the missionaries in the time of Saints Boni-
face and Patrick, they had crossed the deserted expanse of
the Russian plain without encountering a living soul.

They hadn't eaten for several days. We immediately gave them some bread baked in the hearth of a peasant home.

Then we went to find quarters in a village southwest of Kalinin. We first tried to gather a supply of oats for the winter, a share of which was taken from each of the surrounding villages. I made the acquaintance of a man who had been a gamekeeper under the czars, and who had, some years earlier, also participated in a hunt organized by Marshal Kliment Voroshilov himself. On many occasions we went hunting together on a sleigh, wrapped in the same fur blanket, through the vast zone of marshland and peat bogs southeast of the village. Lulled by the peaceful rhythm of this new life in a frozen countryside, somewhat enervated by long sessions in the sauna and by lengthy card parties around the gigantic brick stoves that formed the center of the Russian cottages, we allowed ourselves to be overcome by the conviction that the war would soon be over. When in early December, I saw my gamekeeper for what turned out to be the last time, he greeted me and said, "I'll see you tomorrow; we're going to meet for our little ducks! Agreed?" So convinced were we that the war was over and that we had no reason to be concerned about our new life. Our awakening was brutal.

7

A Christmas in Hell

DECEMBER 1941–JANUARY 1942

On November 20, 1941, Major Hirsch, who had been assigned to another command, left the Sixth Reconnaissance Battalion, and my brother succeeded him as commandant. Projects were arranged to make intelligent use of the winter. Georg thought of giving Latin courses, and procured grammar books and dictionaries, and the staff launched literary and culinary competitions. Four officers, eighteen noncommissioned officers (NCOs), and some enlisted men were sent to Germany for training. Planning for leave was begun, because many soldiers had not seen their families all year.

At the end of November, the temperature fell below −10°C (14°F) during the night. On November 16, it fell to −16°C (3°F) in the evening. We saw the first cases of frostbite, and the doctors, assisted by Russian women, taught the men how to treat them: with delicate massage, applications of talcum powder, warming the affected limb. By mid-December, the daytime temperature had fallen to below −20°C (−4°F). The soldiers had still not received any winter clothing and equipment.

Georg's battalion had been promised four hundred pairs of skis, which finally arrived in the middle of the winter. But the men had only their thin uniform jackets. In December the whole of the Sixth Division received just a few dozen pairs of fur-lined boots and overcoats. The doctors advised the men to wear all their available underclothes. But this was not sufficient. The smallest gaps in the clothing were stuffed with newspaper, packaging materials, and rags; newspaper in one's shorts, newspaper around one's legs and torso. Since they were receiving nothing in the way of official supplies, Georg decided to do something. He sent our friend Karl von Wendt to Westphalia, accompanied by a small team of men and trucks, intending to bring back furs and warm garments.

So there was the battalion in the snow, like a marmot ready to hibernate, thinking more about holing up in a comfortable bivouac than about the possibility of exposure to the cold, and more about celebrating Christmas than about fighting. However, December marked the beginning of the Russian counteroffensive to relieve Moscow. This strategic maneuver, which coincided with the entry of the United States into the conflict, clearly represented a change in the course of the war. It signaled

the end of the German advance into Russian territory in
1941, even if, we thought, that development was not yet
decisive for the outcome of the conflict. The war would
be long; German troops would turn out to be danger-
ously exposed and their immune systems fragile, particularly under such inhuman meteorological conditions.

In mid-December, the situation no longer allowed
the Ninth Army to maintain its bridgehead at Kalinin.
Soviet divisions, perfectly equipped, crossed the frozen
Volga without difficulty, and some units were able to
make impressive inroads, penetrating far beyond the
front lines. Several German divisions were in real danger
of being surrounded and destroyed. A Siberian cold had
set in: the temperature fell to −30° and −40°C (−22° and
−40°F). The wind blew in gusts that almost toppled the
men. And even when the skies cleared and a pale sun
made the white desert shine with a crystalline brilliance,
the beauty of the countryside could not make us forget
the cold, which became even more lacerating.

On December 15, the battalion commanded by Franz-
Josef von Kageneck had held, virtually alone, the road to
Kalinin against forces ten times larger, and thus allowed
almost a whole army to escape being surrounded. In the
early morning of December 16, Georg's reconnaissance
battalion, which was under the command of the Sixth
Army, was ordered to begin withdrawing to the east bank
of the Volga. More unfavorable conditions could not be
imagined. The storm was howling. The snow was

already impressively deep when the men awoke and a terrible, biting wind was raising great spumes of white powder. Drifts blocked the roads. The heavy squadron was struggling: the bad weather was tripling fuel consumption. In the early afternoon, headquarters was informed that the motorized vehicles could not continue farther than twenty-five kilometers without additional fuel. Once again, horses constituted the only reliable mobility in a winter setting. The superior officers were on the brink of despair, but young officers like Georg and Kageneck yielded less to somber reflections. It was a matter of survival. Galvanized by the danger, they often took the initiative.

On December 18, Georg and his men were supposed to secure a 7.5-square-kilometer zone to allow the infantry's relatively orderly retreat from the area between the Tma and the Volga, which they had conquered at the end of October. The enemy pressure was strong, but thanks to their mobility, our troops were able to deceive the Soviets and confuse their scouts. The men had to deal not only with heavy fire but also with the cold. The gusts of wind, which were asphyxiating, burned the lungs. The cold was not only bitter, it was deadly: it could kill a man in a few minutes. If it didn't kill the man whole, it killed his limbs—hands, arms, legs—and the most prominent parts of the face—the ears and the nose. The conditions of the retreat did not allow for the proper burial of the dead. It was impossible to dig graves; instead, the dead were buried under huge piles of snow. On December 24, the temperature fell to −46°C (−50°F).

That day, Siberian troops staged a mass attack on the battalion's cyclist squadron. After inflicting heavy losses among enemy forces that were still poorly equipped, it was possible to stabilize the situation. We had suffered a serious reversal. One thing reassured us: the enemy was losing on average ten to twenty times as many men as we were. But we were now certain that their numbers were immense, and that was their great potential. Beyond that one certitude, how many questions there were! How could the Russian generals let their men be mowed down in such numbers by machine-gun fire? Why didn't they see that their counteroffensive, although it had resulted in clear successes, made no sense? In our opinion, it was a Pyrrhic victory.

When Christmas came, the Sixth Infantry was licking its wounds and counting its losses, which had been considerable over the past fortnight. In theory, Georg's reconnaissance battalion numbered more than a thousand. But on December 27, it was no more than a shadow of its former self. Georg sent his superiors a report explaining that his combat potential had been reduced by 90 percent since June. The cavalry squadron now had only 1 officer, 32 men, and 4 light machine guns. The heavy squadron had only twenty-nine soldiers under the command of a single officer. Finally, the lieutenant who commanded the cyclist squadron had only twenty-two fighters. It is true that several dozen men were on furlough or in training, but since June, the dead and wounded had not been replaced. The battalion as a whole now counted only half as many troops as the squadron that Georg had commanded up until the spring of 1941 . . . and the remaining forces were exhausted because the Soviets were attacking day and night.

On December 29, the enemy launched a new offensive between the Volga and the Tma. The front line was no longer tenable, and our troops had to retreat and take up positions more to the southwest, not far from Rzhev. That city, located where the Volga begins a vast, meandering curve to the north, was an industrial center of about fifty thousand inhabitants, and especially a major railway junction. It could not be left in Russian hands. The 110th, the 126th, and the Sixth Infantry divisions gathered in this sector, where our defense was organized around what was soon to be called the Königsberg position.

On January 1, Georg went to meet the Third Battalion of the Eighteenth Infantry Regiment, which formed the rear guard of the retreating Sixth Division. Its commandant, Kageneck, had died three days earlier. Georg found exhausted men, officers on the verge of a nervous breakdown after countless nights without sleep and weeks without rest. While the soldiers, who were not very close to the defensive line, continued their march, Georg took the officers to his command post to tell them briefly how the Königsberg position was organized. "It is not an ideal front line, but it respects the tactical imperatives and has certain potentialities," he said. "Now, that's not all. Sit down for a moment. I've got a quart of nice hot bouillon for you," he continued with his usual liveliness, even though the Russians were only a few kilometers away. One officer got up to serve. "No," Georg said, shaking his head in protest, "I'll serve today." That was the way my brother was, mixing discipline, lucidity, and good-heartedness.

The front was being stabilized. Rzhev was finally lost only in March 1943, after very fierce fighting. But until the beginning of March 1942, the Russian harassments were incessant, while full-scale attacks came almost daily—dreadful butcheries, the unfurling waves of men drunk on vodka and the cold, cut down by machine-gun fire, but each time reducing our resistance a little. In February, a Russian cavalry division, with the help of partisans, managed to penetrate our rear and create a pocket of territory along the railway from Vyaz'ma to Moscow that was completely outside our control.

The situation in my sector was no better. But the story of my adventures at the turn of the year 1941–42 is briefer than that of the episodes Georg was involved in during those bloody weeks, because a wound I'd received during the first hours of combat, which nearly cost me my life, sent me away from the front. Since the beginning of December, fighting had raged around Moscow, and the

Eighty-sixth Division had been violently torn out of its torpor. On December 10, it was decided to retake a town called Ignatovo, which the Russians had seized. An artillery regiment had left a valuable part of its equipment there. The temperature was now −42°C (−43°F). The cyclist squadron, commanded by Lieutenant Blomberg, was to attack from the south, supported by three heavy machine guns, an antitank gun, and a light cavalry mortar.[1] My cavalry squadron was assigned to lead the attack from the north. We first had to go around the village on the west and through the forest. The snow was so deep that it blocked the antiaircraft gun and the cavalry mortar. Only our heavy machine gun made it to the site.

A merciless battle began that was to last several hours. The Russians resisted stubbornly. Despite the cover provided by artillery camouflaged in a nearby forest—and which unfortunately once landed a shell among our own troops—we were not able to reach the houses on the village outskirts. We had to fight for a house, a fence, a vegetable garden. The enemy firepower dramatically increased and was concentrated on the northern sector. This shift in the Soviet defenses seemed to me inexplicable, although it was tragically simple: the German head adjutant, who was supervising the telephone connection and at the same time commanding the artillery battery, hadn't received the message ordering the division to retreat. The Russians, finding the pressure on their south and west flanks relieved by the departure of the cyclists, had shifted all their efforts to the cavalry squadron, which, kneeling or crawling in the snow as the light faded, persisted in a vain attempt to move forward. It was at that point that a searing pain flattened me. I had been hit in the abdomen. I didn't have much time to think about my fate or even to suffer, because I lost consciousness. When I came to, I managed to stay on the battlefield for a while. The situation was becoming increasingly desperate. Grenades were exploding in the icy snowdrifts, throwing up little columns of snow and powder along with bits of wood and glass. The wounded men's cries of pain, mixed with the crackling of machine-gun fire, shattered the late afternoon; as if through the fog of a slow nightmare, the sound managed to reach my consciousness, despite the blood I'd lost, and despite the sensation of both immense weakness and a certain light-headedness that comes with being seriously wounded. Snow began to fall, heavy, thick, and abundant, but it did not mute the din of the fighting. Soon the light machine guns began to jam. Only the horses were still going about their task, heroic, impassive, moving out damaged equipment and wounded soldiers.

The squadron had already lost thirty-five men. I was wounded again, this time in the left shoulder. I nonetheless had the strength to give the order to retreat at nightfall. The few dozen men who were still on their feet, helped by the inexhaustible horses, hurriedly loaded up the equipment, the wounded, and the frozen bodies of the dead, and set out to look for the battalion, whose location they no longer knew. It seems that they walked for hours in the fresh snow, carrying me on a stretcher. The scouts were in the lead, and were sinking thigh-deep in the snow. The men were stumbling with fatigue, but got up again when they came in contact with the wet snow or were scratched by the ice.

I owed my survival solely to the attention of my men and to the devotion of one adjutant in particular. During the night, we ran into the battalion's physician, who gave me first aid and dressed my wounds. "Lieutenant," he said, "to have any chance of surviving, you must not eat anything for the next several days. Absolutely nothing!" He gave me an entire carton of cigarettes to ward off hunger, and loaded me on a sleigh driven by a Russian prisoner. This man, who had been captured a month earlier, was one of those Russians who viscerally rejected communism and hoped that a German victory would mean a return to the old order. For ten days he drove me over the icy plain. He was a teacher and spoke a little German, but my physical condition prevented me from conversing much with him.

At the Syschevka railway station I was loaded—and that is the right word—onto a freight train, along with forty-two other seriously wounded men. The train remained for three whole days at the station in Orel, without any care or food being given to the wounded. The moans ceased, one by one. Half of the wounded died of the cold. Aerial attacks on the station killed a number of men. I, however, escaped with a piece of shrapnel in my right knee the first night, and another in my left tibia the following night. The few survivors were taken on to Smolensk. There we were transferred, in another freight train, to Germany. I had eaten practically nothing since December 10. The train's engineer occasionally gave me a little something to drink. That was how I spent my Christmas 1941. Finally, after eighteen days' travel, I was taken off the train in Silesia and moved, half dead, to the hospital in Breslau. I had survived about three weeks of transportation and privations—a miracle. Once I had recovered, I drew from all of this very pessimistic conclusions regarding the ability of the military command to conduct the war.

For his part, Georg had not been seriously wounded. He was exhausted, but his morale was intact. He had, I think, lost none of his bravery, his energy, or his presence of mind. He had never considered the situation hopeless, despite the cold, despite the adversary's firepower. With the same gaiety, he continued to give his entourage that impression of invulnerability that made him seem almost a mythical hero. Georg was perfectly well aware of the danger. But he was motivated by a sense of duty that obliged him to show a tranquil optimism. The Russian offensive had lost some of its vigor, and Georg was prepared to fight for every inch of terrain.

But something inexplicable happened. On January 10,

1942, he received, by way of the division, the news that he had been transferred to the Führer's reserve, effective immediately. He was to return to Germany without delay. Georg had not requested this assignment. He was furious to be separated from his men, who owed him everything and to whom he was linked by a set of obligations and loyalties that were as strong as those between a father and his children. Georg tried not to show his bitterness; on January 12, he named his successor and left for Potsdam-Krampnitz, where he was to teach military tactics to elite troops. It is true that from an operational point of view, the cavalry had become less useful. The defensive positions the German army had taken up around Rzhev could be held by the infantry.

At the end of January, Georg and five of his comrades were decorated by the Führer in person. Georg was the fifty-third soldier in the Wehrmacht to receive the Iron Cross with Oak Leaves. At that time he had only disdain for Hitler—not yet hatred. A photo shows the scornful way my brother looked at the Führer. Hitler asked him if he had a special request. Far from thinking of himself, Georg took advantage of the opportunity: "I have heard that my brother Philipp has been seriously wounded. I don't know where he is. Could inquiries be made at the various hospitals?"

The message was immediately sent out in all directions. When the hospital in Breslau realized that I was the wounded man being sought, the doctor came to ask

January 1942, Hitler's headquarters at Rastenburg,
East Prussia: decoration of (from left to right) Hans
Jordan, Karl Eibl, Günter Hoffmann-Schönbron, Georg von
Boeselager, and Karl-Heinz Noak. This allowed Philipp,
who was seriously injured in December 1941, to be
taken back to a hospital in eastern Germany.

me—as in a fairy tale—if I wanted anything. I was by then capable of understanding the situation, and seizing my chance, I asked to be transferred to Bonn. The Führer's wishes were commands, and my request was immediately granted. So I was taken home in a luxurious railway car, in the almost maternal care of two nurses reserved for me. I spent several months in the hospital. When I got out, in spring 1942, I was still convalescent.

A few months later, in July 1942, after the training session was over, Georg was sent to Romania as part of the German military mission. He was supposed to help toughen up the Romanians, whom the Wehrmacht was then using as auxiliaries on the Russian front.

8

The Conspiracy Begins

1941–42

I had not become an officer in order to shoot the head of state like a dog. Desiring the end of the regime and the death of its leader was, in the eyes of our compatriots, not only a state offense but also a stab in the back of the people as a whole, united in fighting a merciless war. The decision to join the resistance could result only from a long deliberation, which was certainly made easier by the events, scenes, and situations I had observed or experienced. Without generalizing from my own case, there were few examples in Germany, at least among military men, of a spontaneous and impulsive commitment to the struggle against the regime. In my case, it was a combination of different experiences that led to the decision to rebel, to the point that this idea, at first difficult to accept, by 1942 seemed obvious and even obligatory. I was also lucky enough to meet people who were further along in this process, and who embodied my commitment. The education Georg and I had received was certainly not alien to the evolution of our views, which advanced in tandem even though we had been separated in 1941–42, and our communications on this subject were necessarily fleeting.

What was our state of mind before we became aware of the need to act? Here is an example taken from June 1941, in the middle of the offensive. My unit was stationed somewhere on the west bank of the Dnieper. Late one evening, I began talking with an artillery lieutenant who was passing through and to whom I had offered hospitality. It was one of those long conversations, frequent among officers, that take place over a last cup of coffee or a glass of liqueur, in which one speaks about his feelings, hopes, and also fears. Our conversation turned to the Nazis, and more precisely to Hitler. Sensing that we were in agreement on the subject, and emboldened by some feeling of mutual trust, by fatigue, and perhaps by a little alcohol, we began to criticize the Führer. We talked about this and that, while the fire burned down. The embers were glowing, and it grew colder. One of us yawned, putting an end to the discussion as spontaneously as we had begun it.

We wished each other good night and went back to our tents. I suddenly broke out in a cold sweat. Who was this fellow with whom I had spoken a bit too frankly? I didn't know him; he belonged to another division, and an artillery division to boot. How could I be sure of his discretion? On the contrary, he had given me every reason to think that he liked to talk. How could I assure myself of his loyalty? Impossible. The army, like all of German society after eight years of dictatorship, was full of informers, swarms of zealous agents loyal to the system. This fellow with a friendly face could very easily betray the feelings of confidence he inspired. Thinking, expressing doubts, mocking the Führer, questioning the meaning of this ideological war was already a crime. My doubt became anguish, and fear yielded to panic. I didn't sleep a wink that night. The following day, I did not attempt to see this dangerous fellow again.

I ran across him, however, a few months later. In the meantime I had learned that he was Achim Oster—the son of Hans Oster, the number two man in the Abwehr, the German counterespionage service, and the keystone of the resistance movements.[1]

"If you only knew how scared I was!" I told him when we had recognized each other.

"And what about me? I didn't sleep all night!"

We laughed a great deal about it, showing how much officers were tempted to express their bitterness in private, despite the danger of doing so, even outside the Nazi apparatus.

At the same time, Georg found himself, according to his comrades, in a similar state of mind. By the end of August 1941, the effects of the disastrous hygienic conditions that had been endured for ten weeks were beginning to make themselves felt among his troops. Exhausted by lack of sleep, confronted by extreme weather conditions, harassed by marches and battles, attacked by lice and mosquitoes, prevented from doing laundry regularly, dozens of men in the Sixth Reconnaissance Battalion were beginning to show the symptoms of dysentery. Despite the strict instructions given by the physicians to drink boiled water and nothing else, the men's bodies, of which too much had been demanded, became vulnerable. Repeated vaccinations carried out in early August against all sorts of epidemics proved insufficient. The weather, which had been so good in early July, had deteriorated. The coolness and humidity at the end of the summer led to cramps and rheumatism among even the toughest. These joint pains, soon accompanied by gastric problems and weight loss, were the early signs of dreadful diarrhea. In short, by August 26, in Georg's cavalry squadron alone, thirty-two men had already fallen sick and were incapable of fighting. Dr. Haape, the physician for the neighboring Eighteenth Infantry Regiment, tried to treat every new case. Georg was ill, even though he refused to be put on the sick list. He did, however, consent to being treated for a week by Dr. Haape, to take laxatives, and even—the greatest shame—to stay in bed for days with a hot-water bottle on his stomach. To thank the doctor, who was indefatigably performing his duties, Georg, who had recovered after eight days under his care, invited him to dinner along with Franz Joseph von Kageneck. They began to talk about this and that. The conversation then turned to more serious subjects. Georg felt at ease talking with Dr. Haape, whose humanity appeared on his round and jovial face (and who related the following conversation to me), and with Kageneck, who was a military man par excellence, a Catholic—he came from a family in Baden that included Metternich's mother—and irreproachably upright.

Soon, Georg gave free voice to his anger against Hitler: "That obtuse parvenu! He's a cheap café politician pretending to be a genius!" he suddenly exploded. "Why didn't he stay in the background and let the generals think for him?"

"Because he is inspired," Kageneck said slowly.

"Do you know what inspiration is?" Haape asked. "It's an intestinal wind that rises by mistake to the head and lodges there—and that's Immanuel Kant's definition, not mine!"

"We can't go on much longer, considering him and his revelations to be just a joke," Georg grumbled, without even smiling at the physician's quip.

The criticism Georg formulated was in fact already quite common among military officers. But Georg went much further. Lowering his voice and leaning over the table, he added, "The Nazis are destroying the heart of the true Germany! When the war is over, it will be people like us who will have to act!"

"But whom will you have to help you?" Kageneck asked doubtfully.

"Most of the generals! From all these discussions something will eventually materialize—particularly if we have to suffer defeats."

"Generals don't make an army," Kageneck interrupted. "You know as well as I do that most of the young officers coming in are confirmed Nazis."

"And what about the troops?" Haape added. "Most of them are happy just to have a place to lay their heads and rations three times a day! They won't do anything. They don't care whether they are fighting for the true Germany or Hitler's Germany. . . ."

Georg was not one to acknowledge self-doubt, to resolutely question himself, to sound out his fellows, to probe the depths of his thoughts, to ask others to confirm them. . . . When he expressed himself, he had already made up his mind. His friends had pointed out the practical difficulties involved in what he proposed. Their objections gave him food for thought, particularly regarding the generals' involvement. But he was already fully committed to his enterprise, even if its exact outlines were not yet clearly determined.

Fifteen months later, Major General Henning von Tresckow enlisted Georg among the opponents and conspirators of Army Group Center. In the meantime, his opinion of Hitler had become more radical, to the point that in his view it was not possible to wait until the end of the war to eliminate him.

I cannot reconstitute the reasoning that led him to this conclusion, the totality of the feelings, analyses, images, and impressions that moved him to take this decisive step. But it is clear that Georg's assignments, starting in early 1942, left him time to observe and meditate. Chance—some would say Providence—had provided him with this strange interlude, this inexplicable parenthesis in a life that up to then had always tended toward action. Established seventy kilometers north of Bucharest, he was the only German among a population that was almost entirely Romanian. In his letters to a female friend of ours, he described his occupations:

> My activity here is not very exciting. I work at the officer training school, where I serve as a supervisor and offer advice regarding the best training methods. The Romanians are extremely sensitive, and one must therefore always be very careful. In other respects, they are very hospitable, and we get along very well. I am trying to train a young dog who is excessively fearful—one of my bitch's puppies. Not ideal for here, because for big game one obviously needs a somewhat more aggressive dog.[2]

Headquarters of Army Group Center, summer 1942:
Philipp, sitting, in his duties as an orderly;
Captain Bülow, standing.

In a later letter he added, "I've quite a lot of time for reflection and writing."[3] Georg was in regular contact with the front by mail, since the postal service was still working well—and people were in the habit of writing to one another often, not only within the family, but also among fellow officers. We also communicated via telephone. I could, in fact, be reached quite easily, given my service to Field Marshal hans Günther von Kluge. And I communicated to Georg all the information I possessed that came from the various divisions. This news, put into perspective during his long periods of leisure, increased his skepticism.

In my own journey the inevitable and the predestined probably played a role. In retrospect, my involvement may seem to have been governed by a logical sequence, but I have to admit that it depended to a great extent on fortuitous circumstances. If I hadn't been wounded in December 1941, if I hadn't been assigned to Kluge's staff, if I hadn't met Tresckow, that exceptional figure, and especially if I hadn't acquired the habit of confiding some of my thoughts to him, I would never have emerged from my reserve. I would have remained captive to private scruples and insoluble internal conflicts. To begin this intellectual and moral development was to embark upon a pilgrimage whose goal was uncertain. It was already to commit treason. To be sure, Hitler had failed many times to keep his word, and he had sacrificed tens of thousands of lives to his diabolical whims. Nonetheless, for a military man, for whom the first requirement was obedience, starting down this road was certainly not easy.

During this period I was very busy, but I also had time to discuss things with other officers, to meditate on the course of events and the regime's goals. That is how a kind of maturation took place in me before more decisive experiences thrust me into active military resistance. Among soldiers, there was much discussion of the sermons that Monsignor Clemens August von Galen, the bishop of Münster, had given against euthanasia almost a year earlier, in the summer of 1941; his vehemence had led the government, contrary to all expectations, to put an end to the T4 program for the eradication of the handicapped.* These sermons had resonated with soldiers, who, after a wound or an amputation, were likely to be grouped with those allegedly useless people. I had not read the sermons, but I had heard many people talk about them, and I had listened all the more attentively because Monsignor Galen, in addition to being my distant cousin, was a compatriot. The bishop was highly regarded among officers with any sense of morality, and his influence on the resistance in the military can be seen in a brief exchange I had with Colonel Hans Oster of the Abwehr toward the end of 1942. Knowing my connection to the Rhineland and Westphalia, and although he was himself a Lutheran, he asked me about the prelate:

---

*Hitler ordered the T4 program halted on August 24, 1941, but some local officials continued killing people with disabilities until the end of the war.

"Are you a relative of Monsignor Galen?"

"No, not really. . . ."

"Too bad. He's a man of courage and conviction. And what resolution in his sermons! There should be a handful of such people in all our churches, and at least two handfuls in the Wehrmacht! If there were, Germany would look quite different!"

In this context, certain incidents led me to enter the conspiracy. In retrospect, compared with the horror of the war and the magnitude of the Nazis' crimes, these incidents seem minor. Another person might have reacted coolly to these experiences, and not been affected by them. But for me, they served as a catalyst. It is time to tell about them.

9

An Encounter with the Demon

JUNE 1942

By early May 1942, I had largely recovered from my wound, but I remained handicapped. Limping, unable to ride a horse, I could not resume an operational assignment. I was therefore attached to the staff of Army Group Center, as aide-de-camp to Field Marshal Kluge. My role, like that of aides-de-camp in every army in the world, varied between all-purpose handmaiden and office manager: handling the marshal's schedule, accompanying him, participating in discussions, writing up reports on meetings, summarizing the dispatches and radio messages that had come in overnight so they could be read in the early morning, running errands, transmitting orders, and, in short, organizing the marshal's material life in order to facilitate his direction of operations. Kluge did not mistreat me. On the contrary, he was concerned about making full use of my abilities. The marshal, who was overloaded if anyone ever was, often asked me to write the orders for the following day—a function that obviously belonged to the operations officer, namely, Tresckow. The next day, the marshal compared Tresckow's orders with mine, and to train me he pointed out my errors and their possible consequences. . . . In the afternoon, when nothing special was planned, we took tea together. In the evening I joined him on his walks. I had, in a way, become the confidant of this old military man, who was a very interesting person.

I was lodged in the same group of huts as Kluge, along with General Wöhler, who was the chief of staff, and the service personnel (the orderly, the cook, and the driver), while the rest of the staff lived in a barracks about three hundred meters away. We went on duty at 6:00 a.m. At that hour we received the night bulletin from the staff's operations office. I was supposed to present it to the marshal at exactly 7:00 a.m. During the first weeks I found this exercise very difficult. On his 1/300,000 map, Kluge had marked only the front, with a thick, dark line. He had not indicated the limits of the respective sectors held by the divisions. At that time Army Group Center included ninety divisions, and I was supposed to indicate, using a long wand, exactly where the night's battles— thrusts, captures, attacks—had taken place, and continue my analysis down to the level of the regiment and the village. Fortunately, I had good eyes. After this presenta-

Kluge's office at Smolensk.

tion came breakfast, which the marshal and I always ate separately, whereas we shared the other meals with the marshal's staff. In the course of the morning, General Wöhler, the chief of staff; Tresckow, the operations officer; the intelligence officer; and other department heads came in to report. That was the routine on sedentary days. However, weather permitting, we boarded a plane several times a week to inspect the terrain. Then it was the local staff's turn to make their reports. Kluge took advantage of this opportunity to visit frontline units directly exposed to the enemy.

The first incident that eventually led me into the resistance occurred a few days after my arrival at the marshal's headquarters, probably in June 1942, though I am unable to determine the exact date. Until I was wounded, I had always been in advance positions, assigned to operational duties. I'd had no opportunity to observe what was happening in the areas of the East that were not under military command, and where the general commissioner, the SS, and the Sicherheitsdienst (SD) exercised an unlimited authority. The military, in fact, had authority over the front—hundreds of kilometers long—and a zone two hundred to three hundred kilometers wide constituting the army's rear (*rückwärtiges Heeresgebiet*). Between that zone and Germany's borders was the buffer zone under the control of the infamous Reichskommissariat Ost. In the territory under military command, the SS was authorized to act only in the

Departure of Army Group Center general staff for a tour of the battlefield (September 1942). General Wöhler is standing; Field Marshal Kluge is in the front passenger seat; Philipp is in the middle of the back seat.

framework of the battle against partisans. This accommodation to the Nazi universe might seem to be a criminal weakness, a cowardly pliability on the part of a hypocritical military hierarchy, which was blind and mute. But the partisans were conducting a merciless guerrilla war in the rear areas. Ambushes; attacks on food supply convoys; massacres of columns of wounded men being taken to the hospital; terrorist actions in villages and farms that had supported us or simply offered us lodging; infiltration of spies along the front lines, sometimes even within the families where the Wehrmacht's soldiers were billeted: all of that not only threatened to disrupt the front, but might also lead to a breakdown of the army's supply chain, which was already extremely vulnerable.

One fine day in the spring, therefore, I received one of the many dispatches I was supposed to summarize for the marshal. This one came from SS Obergruppenführer Erich von dem Bach-Zelewski. It pertained to the rear zone that was beyond military control, but concerned the staff of Army Group Center because it provided information on the actions the partisans had carried out against roads, viaducts, and bridges that had obvious strategic importance. The message ended with what seemed to me an enigmatic and vaguely troubling entry: "Special treatment for five Gypsies." I couldn't grasp the relation between this point and the other rubrics in the message. A few hours later I submitted my report to the marshal,

July 1942: Kluge on the battlefield; Philipp is at right.

and came to the final point: "Marshal, I cannot explain the meaning of this expression."

The marshal replied, "Frankly, I don't know what to tell you. We have to clarify this matter. The simplest way is to ask Bach-Zelewski for further details. As it happens, I have a meeting with him in a few days."

Erich von dem Bach-Zelewski was not harmless. People trembled at the mere mention of his name. He was in his forties, a massive, rather ordinary-looking man. He was very experienced in military affairs, and no one could accuse him of incompetence in that domain. But his service record did not inspire respect. Having entered the army when he was very young, during the last years of the Great War, in 1918–19 he had allowed himself to be drawn into the activities of the *Freikorps*. There he had lost his values and any sense of humanity.[1] Since June 1941 he had been high commandant of the SS and the police (Höherer SS und Polizeiführer) in the central Russia sector. He reigned like a satrap over a sinister empire that included Minsk and Mogilev. Ruthless, coldly calculating, he was truly a creature of the devil.[2]

Among the army's officers, Bach-Zelewski had a scandalous reputation as an unscrupulous careerist who was full of bitterness toward the military men who had expelled him from the army fifteen years earlier. But in the spring of 1942, news of the atrocities committed by his henchmen had not yet spread beyond the limited group of eyewitnesses. Moreover, in the sulfurous rumors that swirled about him, it was hard to distinguish fiction from reality. In any case, he had been assigned to carry on the battle against the partisans that the regular army, which was busy holding the front, could not handle. Erich von dem Bach-Zelewski was thus an unavoidable partner.

I was present at the discussion between Bach-Zelewski and Kluge. They talked first about the guerrillas: how to limit their range, how to eliminate them from the countryside, and especially how to secure the vital connections with Germany. A discreet reminder on my part, once the technical presentation was complete, caused Kluge rather abruptly to ask the SS officer, "Oh, by the way, I was about to forget: What do you mean in your report by 'special treatment'? You apparently gave 'special treatment' to five Gypsies."

"Those? We shot them!"

"What do you mean, shot them?! Following a trial before a military tribunal?"

"No, of course not! All the Jews and Gypsies we pick up are liquidated—shot!"

The marshal and I were both taken aback. I felt the kind of internal dislocation and devastation that leads to panic. Obviously, we sensed that something was wrong. Kluge could not have been unaware that crimes, major crimes, had been committed in areas under his authority. Still, we had attributed them to the uncontrolled excesses of the SS. But here was Bach-Zelewski stating a doctrine of extermination as though it were perfectly natural. What we had taken to be terrible blunders were, in reality, part of a coherent, premeditated plan. The shooting of Jews and Gypsies turned out to be a commonly shared war goal. According to the SS, the instructions were clear and came from the highest level of the government. The marshal got a grip on himself and controlled the trembling of his voice: "But why did you shoot them? You're only creating new partisans by killing them like that. It's incredible! Are you really executing them outside the military code of procedure, without trial?"

The atmosphere became more heated. The old marshal, even though used to dealing with Nazi high officials, was on the verge of exploding. The placid coolness of our interlocutor, his quiet hatred, and simply his way of expressing murderous obsession so calmly may have enraged the marshal even more than the fate of the five unfortunate Gypsies. Overwhelmed by anger, and no doubt emboldened by my presence, he protested in the name of the Geneva convention, the laws of war, and even the interest of the German armies. Bach-Zelewski grew angry as well. He was pale, and his eyes were piercing behind his round tortoiseshell spectacles; his expression, which a moment before had been unctuous, hardened. After a few minutes he put an end to the dispute with these dreadful words: "Jews and Gypsies are among the Reich's enemies. We have to liquidate them." And he added, his myopic eyes fixed on Kluge, without any regard for his rank or function, "Yes, *all* the enemies of the Reich, our mission is to liquidate them!"

The threat was thinly veiled. The SS officer turned on his heel and left.

Kluge was not a man to temporize. He immediately called General Franz Halder of the Army General Staff. Leaving aside pointless humanitarian or legal arguments, Kluge tried to prove the inanity of this enterprise, which stiffened resistance instead of breaking it. The only positive result of his energetic complaints was that we no longer heard about Bach-Zelewski. Perhaps he simply stopped reporting his barbaric acts.[3]

This incident changed my view of the war. I was disgusted and afraid. I had already had occasion to wonder about the meaning of this conflict, its strategic pertinence, and the Führer's tactics. Through friends in my division's reserve battalion who had been sent to Stargard[4] shortly after the invasion of Poland, I had heard rumors about the crimes committed by the SS in the conquered areas. We were surprised not so much by these rumors—there were so many young men without morals in the SS units—as by the perpetrators' complete impunity. We told ourselves that this could not go on for long; we considered these atrocities, which were probable but never proven, to be isolated events.

Henceforth, I had the proof of the abomination before my eyes. It was no longer a matter of isolated acts committed by aberrant individuals. It was a rigorous plan that had been sanctioned by the highest authorities. We had to face the facts: the state, as a whole, was riddled with vice and criminality. And the army, by remaining silent, was making itself the system's accomplice. This situation now seems to us blindingly clear, yet it was not so clear for contemporaries, who were convinced that Germany was a model of civilization and that it could not be subjected to either a dictatorship or a murderous totalitarianism.

For several weeks, I remained in a state of deep perplexity. I reported the incident to Tresckow, in whom I liked to confide. But then what should be done? Speak out—to whom? To say what—denounce the perpetrators? Again, to whom? And according to what criteria? The scale of values had been corrupted: Kluge's altercation with Bach-Zelewski had shown clearly enough how the fruit had already been rotting away from the inside.

From then on, I paid more attention to conversations among officers and to allusions I could now decode, and I came to notice that people within the staff knew about the execution of Jews. It was mentioned covertly, with repugnance, and the blame was put on foreign recruits in the SS. One fact in particular was evident, since members of the staff of Army Group Center had witnessed it directly. In October 1941, in Borissov, Latvian SS men had executed thousands of Jews and thrown them into a giant ditch. By chance, two superior officers, Carl-Hans von Hardenburg and Heinrich von Lehndorff, had seen the massacre. Because of bad weather, the plane carrying them was flying at low altitude and the two had observed every detail of this nightmare. Hardenberg, who was then the private aide-de-camp to Field Marshal Fedor von Bock, commander in chief of Army Group Center, had appealed to his superior. The local military commandant was immediately summoned. How could he have allowed such crimes to be committed on the territory for which he was responsible? He would have to answer for this massacre of the innocents. The commandant, confronted with his own cowardice and racked with remorse, committed suicide. This affair caused two of the principal officers of the staff, Tresckow and Gersdorff, to join the resistance. Yet in the spring of 1942, I was still unaware of this radicalization among my great friends, their state of mind, and the double game they were playing.

I soon had another example of how lethal was the effect of prejudices held by the masters of Germany regarding allegedly inferior races. Tresckow had convinced Kluge to send to the Führer a small delegation of Ukrainians who had defected to our side and wanted to set up a buffer state with its own army. Hitler refused to receive them and had the unfortunate delegates immediately shot.

10

An Incident at the Führer's Headquarters

The second incident that contributed to my joining the conspiracy took place at the Führer's headquarters in Vinnytsya,[1] in Ukraine. For very important matters, the marshal called upon the commander in chief. In the summer of 1942, the critical situation in the Rzhev salient already justified a request for an audience. In July, the German army had purged the region's southwest sector of the last Russian troops that had been infiltrated there. But the feeling of security did not last. Since August 1, Rzhev had been under attack by Soviet forces several hundred thousand men strong. The feeling of security did not last. The Soviets, now supplied by the Americans, were using unprecedented firepower. The Ninth Army, under General Walter Model, was now in serious danger of being surrounded—a real mousetrap. Within the structure of Army Group Center, the Ninth Army occupied an important place. Kluge, fearing that it would be completely destroyed, urged that certain positions considered nonstrategic be abandoned, that the front line be shortened to make it more defensible, and especially that the troops that had been fighting nonstop since June 1941 be relieved, allowing them a little rest in the rear area to rebuild their strength. The conversation had been carefully prepared, with a series of arguments, information sheets for the presentation, and so on. I was all the more interested in this issue because I had several friends and cherished cousins in that sector. It was a matter of life and death for my old comrades in the Eighty-sixth Division, and also for my brother Georg's comrades in the famous Sixth Reconnaissance Battalion, which was caught in the same net. Early on the morning of August 9, we flew to Vinnytsya.

For the first time, I was not allowed to take part in the discussion. At lunch, I was separated from Kluge. While he sat at the Führer's table, I was placed at Martin Bormann's. Bormann was the head of the party and the Führer's partner in crime. My first impression of Bormann—brutal, careless, and violent—was of a man who immediately inspired fear. At the table were seated representatives of all the ministries. Although I was surrounded by men in various uniforms, I was among the few genuine military men. These gaudy outfits and tinny decorations seemed to me worthy of a decadent royal court. The conversations I overheard were so dreadfully banal that I remember them perfectly.

Soon after the meal began, the representative of the Foreign Ministry, who wore an elaborate dress uniform, asked Bormann what should be done in the following case: Archduke Joseph, an Austrian marshal, was about to celebrate his seventieth birthday. Should a congratulatory telegram be sent to him? The diplomat pointed out that the marshal had married a Wittelsbach—that is, a Bavarian Catholic (he seemed not to realize that the Habsburgs themselves were Catholic). Bormann peremptorily issued his verdict: "Catholic? Then he won't get his telegram!"

The representative of the Ministry of Agriculture asked Bormann what would happen to the former Soviet collective farms (kolkhozes) that specialized in growing *kok-sagyz,* a local variety of dandelion whose roots could theoretically produce a rubber substitute. Scientific studies would have to be done to confirm the value of growing it. Bormann, half serious, immediately passed the buck, saying only, "That's a matter for Reichsführer Himmler!"

At dessert, some of these gentlemen complained that fresh strawberries were already unavailable in the Führer's headquarters, so that they had had to resort to cherries—which were unpleasant because they had pits.

Finally, a few of them who'd drunk a little too much asked in loud voices who wanted to go that evening to provide gallant company for the girls in the Kraft durch Freude group that was visiting Vinnytsya.

This was too much for me: the gravity of the fate of the Ninth Army had met with moral and intellectual poverty and a disconcerting futility. Without a word, boiling with rage, I left the table and went out to smoke a cigarette to calm down. A few moments later, an aide-de-camp stuck his head out to say "Reichsleiter Bormann is asking for you."

Coffee and liqueurs were being served. Bormann asked me to explain what I had done. I told him how I felt: "As a lieutenant and aide-de-camp to Marshal Kluge, I had imagined the Führer's headquarters differently. I accompanied the marshal to discuss the tragic fate of the Ninth Army, which is surrounded at Rzhev, and here people are talking about strawberries!" My frankness, though clothed in politeness, did not please Bormann. Without answering, he turned around and called hoarsely to an SS man: "Take this guy away." I was locked up nearby in a small room, almost a cell. I thought of the episode in the garage in Bonn, ten years earlier. What was going to happen now? I lit another cigarette.

Having finished his lunch, Kluge was already preparing to leave, in a state of irritation not unlike my own. He came out of the mess hall and looked around for me. I heard him calling me. The guard posted outside the room finally whispered something to the marshal, thereby betraying his boss. Pushing the SS man aside, Kluge tore open the door and demanded, "What are you doing there?" I stammered a few words. The marshal interrupted me: "You'll tell me all about it in the plane. Come on, out of there, we're leaving!" We quickly got into the car, which took us to the aerodrome. During the flight, I told him about my marvelous half day. Kluge concluded, "That's enough, that's enough. This time I was able to save you. The next time, you'll keep your mouth shut. But basically, you're absolutely right!"

11

A Poisoned Gift

My misadventure in Vinnytsya had proven instructive. However, I was constantly asking myself, what could I do, as a young subordinate officer without operational duties? What could I do alone, without support? The answer was to come by itself two months later.

It was October 29, 1942. Hitler had called the marshal, as he often did. I was at my post in the aide-de-camp's office, which was next to the marshal's. I picked up my receiver in order to listen in on the conversation. This was not an indiscretion on my part: I was supposed to listen in on telephone conversations in order to offer my impressions to the marshal and to ensure that there was no misunderstanding. This systematic monitoring shows the degree of mistrust that existed between Hitler and his generals.

As commander in chief, Hitler liked to give his instructions directly to the marshals. Eager for revenge, the little ex-corporal from 1918 wanted to pit his tactical genius against what he regarded as the excessively academic minds of the military professionals. He wanted to tear them away from the comfortable certainties that he viewed as mediocre and pedestrian. He despised these pros, but he needed their expertise and their obedience. Thus, the conversations were always animated by an almost electrical anxiousness. Kluge's operational considerations, which followed a rather classical schema, collided with the Führer's implausible strategic designs—the technician versus the amateur; the pragmatist versus the ruthless aesthete. Kluge never minced words; Hitler sometimes gave his anger free rein. I often believed that when the conversation was over Kluge would be relieved of his command. However, at the last moment, Hitler, with Machiavellian cleverness, managed to avoid a definitive rupture and reduced the tension by an adroit pirouette—a sudden change of subject, a personal compliment. The monster turned the situation around with acrobatic agility. "Oh, by the way," he would say, for example, "I've had your wife sent a bouquet of her favorite flowers, with my best wishes for her birthday. As for the rest, I'll call you back later." Finishing the conversation on an almost friendly note, the dictator then made his decision in private, without consulting anyone else, because he was commander in chief.

A Poisoned Gift

This time, Hitler was calling simply to congratulate the marshal on the occasion of his birthday, which was the following day. He concluded this way: "Marshal, I've heard that you intend to have stables built at Böhne.[1] In consideration of the many services you have rendered to the German people and to me personally, I'm giving you two hundred and fifty thousand marks for construction materials! Happy birthday, and good-bye!"

"*Heil, mein Führer*," the marshal replied automatically.

But Hitler had already hung up. The gift was sumptuous. In a Germany that was completely focused on the war, it was extremely difficult to procure construction materials, especially since 1941 and the beginning of extensive air attacks on German cities, where daily destruction increased the need for wood, cement, and bricks.

The bell rang in my room. I went into Kluge's office. Obviously embarrassed that I had listened to this conversation, he asked, "You heard what the Führer said at the end of his call. Just between us, what do you think about it?"

Despite my efforts to get along with my superior—I was still only twenty-five years old—I answered the sixty-year-old man somewhat coolly: "Marshal, I admit I don't recall that any Prussian marshal ever accepted a present from a sovereign in the course of a campaign. After a victory, yes. But during a conflict, never. If I were you, Marshal, I would give the money to the Red Cross."

Suddenly embarrassed by my temerity, I took my

leave of the marshal, who was stunned. I was afraid that he might bring up this incident later, especially at teatime, but he didn't. When we had finished our tea, I went, pensively, to the officers' wing of the staff headquarters. Had I exceeded the limits of an aide-de-camp's freedom? I asked to see General Tresckow. I knew that I could confide in and almost confess to the staff's first officer, whose human qualities and good sense invited that sort of thing. Tresckow was a discreet man; he would not talk to others about the incident. The staff's workroom was full of people. We retired to a small room next door, where maps were kept. I told him about what had happened and asked his advice, for I had no doubt that the marshal would return to this telephone conversation when we were alone again.

The reaction of Tresckow, who was almost as upset as I was, surprised me. My astonishment grew when he asked my permission to speak with the marshal. I protested energetically: impossible; I knew secrets that I had to protect. We got unusually testy with each other. "Colonel," I said, "I'm an orderly in the personal service of Marshal Kluge. This is a position that requires absolute discretion. You cannot mention our conversation. I came to you as an experienced counselor, not as my superior. Furthermore, the marshal is my only superior."

Tresckow looked at me with a serious air. After a moment's silence, he said to me in a penetrating voice, weighing his two short sentences and speaking slowly in order to be sure he was understood, "The marshal must not make himself dependent on the Führer. We need him in our fight against Hitler." With these few words, Tresckow had unveiled himself. He had at the same time enlisted me in his group of conspirators. I couldn't go backward; he left me no choice. Several times, waiting outside Kluge's office before the morning briefings, we had occasion to exchange double entendres, and he was able to test my mental dispositions. These two very simple sentences now demanded my absolute confidence.

My heart swelled. Filled with an immense feeling of relief, I knew in whom I could confide, and with whom I could act. I was dazed, intoxicated by the trust of this superior officer whose prudence, intelligence, and shrewdness I admired. Tresckow had wrenched me out of the spiral of silence, remorse, fear, and disgust. The filth and blood of the war were no longer my sole horizon. I found hope again.

The next day, Kluge received the staff to celebrate his sixtieth birthday. Assuming that news of Hitler's gift might have gotten out, he put it at the center of the conversation: "What do you think about this little 'tip'?"

Major General Krebs saw no problem in accepting the gift as an equivalent of the fiefs granted under the Kaiser. But Tresckow warned Kluge, imploring him, "I beg you, Marshal, don't accept a penny!"

I repeated my suggestion regarding the Red Cross. I don't know what the marshal decided in the end.

I never considered for an instant not telling Georg about all of this. We were too close. But I had to hold my tongue for a long time. He was in Romania; correspondence was subjected to random censorship. The telephone worked well, but it was not secure. I had to wait until we could see each other. This opportunity came at the end of 1942.

12

The Tresckow Group

1942–44

Tresckow, a Prussian Protestant, was an officer and the
son of an officer. His vigorous soul, faultlessly upright,
radiated from an inner peace that infused his whole way
of being. The strength of his personality, imbued with an
authentic and unostentatious piety, was naturally communicated to those around him. Strict with himself but
not austere with others, Tresckow had not confined himself to a great estate or the Reichswehr's bunkers. Profes-
sional experience in banking and living in Latin America
in the 1920s had given him an openness of mind that was
rare in his milieu. He was a generous man. In a group, his
presence created a natural force of attraction, a magnet-
ism. He never forced people to go along with him; they
came spontaneously, of their own accord. He was one of

those rare individuals who combine kindness, intelligence, and effectiveness.

The experience of war and the proximity of death had not hardened him excessively. He expressed his feelings modestly, loved nature, and was constantly admiring the work of his Creator. One day, we had gone hunting together at dawn. The first rays of sunlight were slowly dissipating the darkness, and the milky clouds were tinted a very pale pink. Nature, in the freshness of dawn, had taken on the first colors of autumn. We heard the hoarse, spellbinding serenading of the stag. Then came the nuptial song of the woodcock, and his proud, grotesque strutting. I aimed my rifle. Tresckow put his hand on my shoulder, stopping me. We took the time to inhale deeply the early morning air, to contemplate Nature's preparations, and to listen to the strange melodies of the animal world. We started out again in pursuit of the woodcock, then stopped to observe in silence multicolored jays hopping around in the great, shady mass of the drowsy forest.

It is difficult to describe a man's faith without descending into hagiographical platitudes. Henning von Tresckow was inhabited by an ardent piety that he was not afraid to express. For Christmas 1942, the general command of the Wehrmacht had forbidden any celebration. Nazi officers had been assigned to see to the observance of this injunction. Thus, it was surprising when Tresckow came silently forward among his men, flanked by Georg Schulze-Büttger and Hans-Ulrich von Oertzen. The operations officer read the Christmas gospel just as he would have done amid his own family. I had informed Kluge of what Tresckow was going to do; thus the marshal had come to the junior officers' mess solely to provide cover for his subordinate. It was a true Christian Christmas, to the joy of the overwhelming majority.

Tresckow had a philosopher's forehead, meditative eyes, and an artist's hands. This soldier loved peace, because he knew what war was. He had tasted its bitterness in 1917, when he enlisted as a cadet at the age of sixteen. In June 1918, he had gone to the front in France as a second lieutenant in the Imperial Guard's prestigious First Infantry Regiment. During the deadly retreat, he had contemplated the distress of people in the combat zones. After the war was over, he had to readapt to civilian life, with the same appetite for discovery. As the operations officer on the staff of Army Group Center since early summer 1941, he had seen the proof of inconceivable atrocities piling up on his desk. A surfeit of corroborating evidence made an unshakeable resolution of the vague project that he had envisaged as early as 1939: to kill Hitler. At first fleeting, the idea that it was up to him to take the initiative had become a deep conviction. For while some generals were ready to act, others, although tempted by the military adventure, were paralyzed by the Prussian tradition of obedience to the monarch.

Tresckow had thus resolved to count on himself and

on younger officers to decapitate the regime. Without overestimating his abilities, he knew he could be both the architect and the brains of the operation, but he needed helpers. He had tried in vain to get his uncle, Field Marshal Fedor von Bock, the commandant of Army Group South, to join him. He had also struck higher up, in the circle of his acquaintances, beginning with Gersdorff. Since the beginning of the 1941 campaign, the two had talked quite freely. Gersdorff was the staff's intelligence officer; in regular contact with the intelligence services in Berlin, toward which a nebulous group of regime opponents led by Admiral Wilhelm Canaris, the Abwehr chief, and Colonel Hans Oster gravitated, he was able to fill out the picture of the massacres, counting up the victims and transmitting these figures to Tresckow and their Berlin counterparts.

Among the subordinate officers, Fabian von Schlabrendorff was, I think, the first one approached. He was Tresckow's aide-de-camp, his cousin, and his junior by five years. A lawyer and the son of a general, he knew what law and justice were. At family reunions before the war, he had shared with Tresckow his conviction that Germany had to be rid of tyrants. His intransigent nature, coupled with a rather contrarian spirit, naturally led him into the Resistance. He and Tresckow formed a complementary pair: if Tresckow was the soldier full of humanity, Schlabrendorff typified the man of law, the civilian in uniform—a uniform that was, moreover, frequently in slight disarray. A courtroom duelist with a sharp tongue, tenacious, caustic sometimes to the point of cruelty, he was not afraid to embarrass an interlocutor or even to wound him. But his intellectual's spectacles and the quibbler's chatter could not hide his heart, nor the freedom of conscience nourished by his faith in God. The austere Schlabrendorff was to maintain an exemplary fidelity to all of us, even under torture.

It had been easy to approach Georg Schulze-Büttger, because his post as head of operations made him Tresckow's closest collaborator on the staff. Schubü—his universally adopted nickname—was a devout Protestant and an indefatigable worker, endowed with an unfailing sense of humor. He was an invaluable member of Tresckow's group; in fact, he had been aide-de-camp to General Ludwig Beck, the former head of the Army General Staff who had resigned in 1938. We envisaged Schubü playing a key role if the coup d'état ever succeeded.

The group was then enlarged by successive recruitments. Tresckow seized opportunities, but left nothing to chance. He never decided to approach an officer without first having observed him attentively. Rejecting any cooptation, he made up his own mind in each case.

At the end of 1942, our group included, in addition to Fabian von Schlabrendorff and me, Carl-Friedrich von Berg-Schönefeld, lieutenant colonels Gersdorff and Kleist (the latter known as Uncle Bernd)[1] and Major Pretzell.

Major Alexander von Voss succeeded Schulze-Büttger. Pretzell was replaced by Hans-Ulrich von Oertzen, who incarnated the cavalry officer par excellence: cheerful, optimistic, elegant, and refined.

By definition the group could not be stable, because any of its members could be transferred to other posts or lose their lives in combat. At that time there were at most thirty committed and resolute conspirators, the largest number of insurgent officers we would ever assemble. None of us wanted to expand the group too much, out of concern for secrecy, but also because we wished to spare lives by compromising as few people as possible. Our group could count on certain intermediaries. I had complete confidence in the aides-de-camp of the commanders in chief of the other two army groups, for they were classmates and horsemen to boot—united by the cavalry's code of honor. With the marshal's authorization, I used the pretext of regular mail delivery to visit the other armies. Completely against regulations, I exchanged maps of the front with my counterparts. Each of the conspirators activated his own network that had been constituted before the war and usually consisted of classmates. Schlabrendorff played a crucial role in the organization of the Berlin network, which was composed of the former chief of staff Beck, Hans Oster, and General Friedrich Olbricht. A trip by Tresckow to the capital would have looked suspicious, whereas the comings and goings of his orderly passed unnoticed.

The Tresckow Group

My participation was valuable for the conspirators. Before the war, I had received, in Höxter's infantry regiment, a kind of training normally reserved for military engineers: how to use explosives. I kept a stock of different kinds, of foreign origin. As a rule, explosives were rare and kept under tight control. All movements of stocks were precisely recorded. It was impossible, even for high-ranking officers in the Wehrmacht, and even within German territory, to divert significant quantities. I, however, was able to procure more or less anything I wanted. When our regiment was set up in April 1943, Colonel Helmuth Stieff had designated it an experimental unit (*Versuchstruppenteil*); this provided me an official justification for my tests, by which I determined that English explosives were the most effective, particularly their detonators. Therefore, I became the conspiracy's chief explosives expert, as it were.

Nothing would be more misleading than to imagine us as a little group of conspirators entirely absorbed in our cause, spending whole nights consulting in a smoke-filled room, remaking the world and planning assassinations. For our meetings, we took advantage of the changing of the guard between day service and night duty. The latter was assigned to officers ranking below captain, and there were not enough of them to go around; I often volunteered. This gave me a pretext for going to Tresckow's bunker. Night duty began at 11:00 p.m., but Tresckow went to bed late, after a ritual chess game that provided an opportunity to discuss his projects with his circle of close associates. The meetings didn't last long; we didn't want to attract attention. We were accustomed to concise orders and exact communications, and we seldom chatted or engaged in collective reflection. At first, nonetheless, we discussed at great length the legitimacy of our mission and the justification for murder— for an assassination, even of a tyrant, remains a murder. Then we came to the practical aspects. Tresckow was full of ideas, and his observations, always correct, were naturally accepted by his comrades. He never spoke as a superior officer, always as a friend, with a paternal gentleness that led us to share his convictions. We would have liked to have him as a simple company captain. For Tresckow it was less a closed group of impassioned conspirators than a breeding ground for men ready to sacrifice their lives, to act at the least signal, to execute his plans without fail. Trust and total availability were our watchwords.

Tresckow was also looking for cover in the military hierarchy. To be sure, the putsch would not come from the generals, but Tresckow wanted at least to be sure that they would keep quiet and wish him well. At the end of 1942, he tried to approach Field Marshal Kluge through Carl-Friedrich von Berg-Schönefeld, the second in command of the intelligence services. While they were both out wolf-hunting, the lieutenant drew the marshal aside and surprised him by asking how he felt about Hitler and then asked what his reaction would be in the event that

Hitler were physically eliminated. Their conversation stopped at that point; the lieutenant reported to Tresckow, who went to see the marshal the next day to inform him of his plans. Kluge exclaimed, "Count on me!" He subsequently limited himself to an attitude of benevolent neutrality, but that was still enough to cost him his life.

The true motivations of the conspiring officers are still the subject of lively controversy in Germany. We are said to have wanted to preserve our conquests in the East at any price, by concluding a separate peace with the Americans and the British that would make it possible to impose harsher conditions on the Soviets once the war effort was directed entirely toward them. We are supposed to have wanted to reestablish Germany's 1914 borders. I categorically deny that claim. Our information left no doubt about the Allies' firm intentions; they would liquidate all the Reich's possessions outside the 1938 borders. One didn't need to be a great strategist to see that the entry of such a great economic power as the United States, spared fighting on its own soil, would tilt the scales sharply in favor of our adversaries. The war was obviously lost, and none of the belligerents had an interest in making a separate peace with Germany. The Casablanca Conference, in January 1943, had, moreover, required Germany to surrender unconditionally. Finally, Hans Oster, the number two man in the Abwehr and a focal point for the various conspiracies, informed us of discussions regarding the fate of German territories that testified to the degree of solidarity among the Allies. For us, it was therefore a question of putting an end to the hostilities and saving as many lives as possible—nothing more.

I recall a conversation that I had with Tresckow and Schulze-Büttger in early 1943. When I asked in a loud voice whether it was still worthwhile, given the military situation, to pursue our assassination plans, Tresckow gravely remarked, "Gentlemen, every day we are assassinating nearly sixteen thousand additional victims. We have no choice."

13

When Horses Make Meetings Easier

1943

The German army had never ceased to use horses in support of the artillery, to substitute for failing machinery on the Russian front, and to aid bogged-down supply columns. Mobile and resilient, horses were often more reliable than motors, and despite exhaustion from the long marches made since summer, they continued to serve numerous purposes. The animals provided for the mounted cavalry could, at a trot, advance at sixteen kilometers an hour, and draft horses at thirteen kilometers an hour. The cold did not take them by surprise. Whereas the men tried to pad their thin uniforms with paper and rags, the horses' hair thickened naturally, becoming almost like fur, to our great astonishment. When hay and oats began to run short on the immense, snowy plains, the horses reacted by tearing off the tenderest branches of the pine trees. They even chewed on the edges of the cottages' thatched roofs when they could reach them. Finally, they developed the habit of sucking icicles for water. Their adaptability was phenomenal.

For the cavalrymen, the horse was a home away from home. Our mounts carried our personal effects (clothing and other articles, toiletries) and the tents—each horseman carried a quarter of the latter. And what tender caresses the men and their animals exchanged after a battle! Obviously, we horsemen were linked by camaraderie, a pact of mutual aid, and the certainty that even if they remained silent, our fellows understood and supported us. But the animals—their hair, their moist muzzles, their shivers—paradoxically provided us with a physical intimacy, a warmth, that we could not allow ourselves even among our best comrades. In the extreme severity of war, the men confided in their horses, depended on them. The horse, for its part, was incapable of surviving without its master's care. And in the end it is hard to say which was the more useful to the other, the horseman or the mount.

For a long time my brother Georg had been thinking about how to harness the tactical potential of the cavalry. On this immense front, it was not firepower and the abundance of matériel alone that would decide the outcome. Furthermore, in such respects, the German army did not have the advantage. With an industrial base damaged by the Depression and now handicapped by air raids, it would never be able to produce as many artillery shells and munitions as it had in 1917. It would never succeed in challenging the superiority of an enemy that the United States had begun providing with armaments. Nor would human resources be able to turn the war around. By this fifth year of the war, those born between 1915 and 1925 had already been decimated. It would be necessary to call upon younger and younger recruits who were hastily trained. The rotation of troops was particularly tragic in the infantry. To sow disorder among the adversary, close the breaches, and cover our retreat, what we needed was mobility, quick reactions, and a more economical use of matériel. In apparently hopeless situations, such as Christmas 1941, Georg's cavalrymen had acted decisively to avoid disaster by galloping toward the rear and setting up a line of defense, and by galloping forward to create chaos among the enemy.

My brother had two models, which, with his fair-minded intelligence and habit of judging solely on the merits, he had chosen among the enemy. Actually, Georg didn't have any enemies, only adversaries: he never expressed either hatred or scorn when speaking of the Russians. His first model was Major General Lev Dovator, commandant of the Red Army's Second Guards Cavalry Corps, which had succeeded in penetrating the German front line on December 13, 1941, cutting off

German communications and supply convoys. Such enthusiasm didn't give Dovator much chance of survival: he was killed a few days later, at age thirty-seven. Georg's second model was General Pavel Belov, who survived the war. In November 1941, while commanding the Soviet Second Cavalry Corps, supported by a tank division, Belov had already routed and repelled several Wehrmacht divisions. In early 1942, with incredible boldness, he had penetrated deep behind the German front line at Dorogobuzh, hooked up with the partisans, and held on until the end of March despite being completely surrounded.

For our cavalrymen scattered over different divisions, the constitution of a specialized regiment was a question of survival. Georg had long meditated on this while in Romania. On December 26, 1942, after a short leave in Heimerzheim, he traveled into the heart of Russia, stopping off to see his comrades in the old Sixth Battalion squadron. Of its officers, the only survivor was Wilhelm König, whom his colleagues had for years called only by his nickname, King. Georg received an enthusiastic welcome from his former subordinates.[1] I had done everything I could to make his journey easier and, since the road to Rzhev passed not far from Smolensk, where Army Group Center was headquartered, I set up an interview for him with Field Marshal Kluge on January 8, 1943. With his particular capacity for conviction, Georg explained to the commander in chief the tactical advantages of the cavalry: its mobility, its swiftness, its indifference to weather conditions, and its ability to harass the enemy out of proportion to its small numbers and modest firepower. Kluge had met my brother before the war, when he was in charge of the Westphalian military region. He had heard about Georg's exploits in France and his spotless military career. He listened in silence. The next day—having slept on it—the marshal said that he had been convinced by my brother's presentation, and was prepared to try out the idea. "Go and work out all the details with Tresckow," he advised Georg.

I organized the meeting. Georg and Tresckow were leaders of men, true tacticians. They were able to judge and assess each other in a few moments; their discussion was brief. In a letter to Georg on July 27, Tresckow summed up their meeting and their intermittent contacts over the next six months: "We have seen each other only a few times, but I think these brief moments are enough for us to know what we are doing together. I will always be loyal to you, and I would be grateful for your loyalty in return. And now, keep it under your hat!"

The two men had resolved to set up an autonomous cavalry force that would serve not only military ends but might also, under Georg's command, be used in the framework of a coup d'état. This force completed Tresckow's arrangements for the overthrow of the regime: in addition to Kluge's approval and a network of officers in whom he could have confidence, he could now count on mobile operational units whose commanders were loyal to him. A great many practical details remained to be dealt with. A few weeks earlier, Colonel Helmut Stieff, another member of our network, had been appointed head of the Army General Staff's Organization Department, and he shared Tresckow's views regarding the dual role of the cavalrymen. Less than a week after his meeting with Georg, Tresckow received Stieff's instructions. On January 14, he could order the immediate regrouping, under Georg's command, of the vestiges of the main cavalry units.

The involvement of Georg's cavalry unit in the group's projects did not remain secret. Franz von Papen, then the German ambassador in Ankara, writes in his memoirs that in April 1943 he had a confidential discussion with Count Wolf von Helldorf, the Berlin police superintendent, and Gottfried von Bismarck, the governor of Potsdam. The latter told him about plots against Hitler in which the cavalry regiment led by Georg von Boeselager, who was mentioned by name, was to capture the head of state and the principal leaders of the Nazi Party. This description, though somewhat distorted by rumor, shows what a dangerous position my brother and I found ourselves in. Fortunately, these three high officials were playing a double game and took care not to inform the Reich's dreaded state security police.

Outside these authorized circles, news of the establishment of a cavalry group spread like wildfire within the little world of the cavalry. On January 25, König and his men had reached Smolensk. Soon thereafter, having been brought into the operation a few weeks later, I left the marshal's service to join them. Georg worked hard to bring in all the usable cavalry squadrons; to provide them with the proper number of horses again; to set up sufficient artillery cover; to provide the units with communications equipment; to re-create support functions from the ground up; and to recruit enough veterinarians, as one of his major concerns was to ensure that the horses would be well cared for. When spring came, the mares gave birth to seventy colts, which were sent, after a few weeks of being suckled, to East Prussia. The horses consumed a great deal of fodder, most of it imported from Germany. A normal-size horse needs five kilograms of straw per day, and the same amounts of hay and oats. We had to procure sufficient feed and especially to get ready for winter. So we constructed a wooden hay press that allowed us to make rectangular bales that would be stored for the cold season. Georg was willing to deal with every detail. He had as much confidence in Field Marshal Kluge as I did, but nothing was simple. He wrote, telephoned, inspected, visited the herds of horses; he observed, judged, weighed. He pestered Berlin with multiple requests, hoping to wear the officials down. The Army General Staff looked with favor on his projects, and Georg had a good contact in Major Claus von Amsberg, the officer charged with supervising the cavalry, whom he had met on the Orient Express the preceding summer on his way to Romania.

Absorbed by his incessant activity, Georg almost forgot to eat and drink; a few eggs, a quart of coffee, or a cup of mocha seemed to be enough for him. He slept only five hours a night. He didn't even have time to ride his own five horses every day; he had entrusted their dressage to Fritz Thiedemann. The only relaxation he allowed himself was to go hunting at dawn, often alone with his dog. Sometimes ranging over the steppe or the forests, sometimes going deep into the marshes, he rediscovered the joys of his youth, hiding in the bushes watching for game. With a rabbit or a fox in his game bag, he came back a few hours later, just as the camp was waking up. His mind cleared, he gave his orders and the day began.

According to Tresckow's instructions, the cavalry group was supposed to have 28 officers, 160 NCOs, 920 troopers, and a few more than 1,000 horses. By the end of February, 350 Cossacks had joined the group; their integration was handled by Captain Fritz-Dietlof von der Schulenburg. The cavalry group, called the Boeselager Reiterverband, was then composed of four cavalry squadrons, a mortar battery, an intelligence detachment, and an artillery squadron. On April 6, the group was transformed into a genuine regiment composed of two battalions. The first was commanded by Captain Walther Schmidt-Salzmann. I took command of the second.

14

The Three Failed Attempts

Only a handful of officers were permitted to be in close proximity to the Führer. Among them were his personal aide-de-camp, Rudolf Schmundt, a classmate of Tresckow's, and, of course, the marshals. But an officer below the rank of general had very few opportunities to approach the dictator and thus to assassinate him. Before any meeting, moreover, one had to remove one's belt and one's sidearm. Thus, Tresckow thought that it would be much easier to eliminate Hitler when he came to visit the Russian front than to seek him out in his impregnable headquarters called the Wolf's Lair (*Wolfsschanze*). But Army Group Center was only one of the three army groups on the eastern front. Moreover, the Führer had a temporary headquarters on the Russian front and hardly moved around among the troops at all. Tresckow nonetheless succeeded in drawing Hitler into a trap. Through Schmundt, he let it be known that Kluge was violently opposed to launching Operation Citadel, the attack on the Kursk salient. To allay the marshal's annoyance, Hitler had to visit the front and restore confidence, if not harmony. The ploy produced its intended effect: the Führer was asked to cajole the marshal, and he was tempted by the amusing prospect of manipulating and converting his detractor. It remained only to set a date for the visit.

We were not sure whether to use a firearm or explosives in our attempt on the Führer's life. The choice of a bomb would limit the opportunities to act, besides causing more casualties beyond Hitler's immediate entourage, including the conspirators themselves. Thus we decided on a pistol—without, however, excluding the possibility of explosives as a fail-safe. The method we adopted did not, for all that, guarantee success. Through Schmundt, Tresckow had learned that the dictator wore a thin bulletproof vest under his uniform. In addition, Baron Gersdorff had observed that the Führer's cap was lined with metal. In short, the assassin would have to aim carefully at some chink in the armor. But we were not well-informed enough to be sure that most shots would kill him. And so we concluded that it would be necessary to shoot him in the face.

We were actively preparing, working out scenarios, practicing our aim. Still, we had to decide who was going to pull the trigger. Shooting somebody in the back already demands a great deal of sangfroid, and shooting him from the front is still more difficult. But shooting someone in the face is something else again. Georg saw Tresckow daily in order to ensure that his cavalry group would have priority. One day Tresckow suddenly asked him straight out whether he was prepared to assassinate the man who had solemnly decorated him a year earlier. My brother was a man of resolute temperament, and hunting had made him a good shot. Tresckow had decided that he wouldn't get rattled. Georg reflected for a moment, and then conceded that he couldn't guarantee hitting his mark. He was not afraid for his life, though indeed a solitary shooter would be completely exposed to the bodyguards' fire. He was afraid that he might get too nervous to aim properly.

He therefore accepted, but only on the condition that he not be alone. There were nine conspirators in all, four from the staff and five from the cavalry unit being formed. Among the former were Captain Schmidt-Salzmann and I. I had delayed for a month taking up my command, which was initially scheduled for March 1, 1943, so as to be able to devote myself more fully to preparing for the assassination attempt. The scenario was as follows: once Hitler had come into the mess hall and sat down for lunch, Georg was to stand up and count "one, two," whereupon the rest of us would also stand up and fire. There would probably be a few bodyguards, but

The officers' dining room where the March 1943
attempt to shoot Hitler was to take place.

they would be on the edges of the room, not seated at the main tables. Obviously, we were expecting them to react, but we were counting on the confusion to render them ineffective. It was as simple as that. Everyone knew exactly his position and his role. It was important that there be several shooters, in case an unforeseen obstacle caught one of the bullets.

We also had a backup plan in the event that the lunch was canceled at the last minute, as Hitler was not fond of banquets. Wilhelm König's cavalry squadron would intercept the Führer while he was passing through the forest and hand him over to an improvised military tribunal, which would sentence him to a firing squad. Finally, as a last resort, Schlabrendorff had proposed putting explosives in the Führer's plane.

It remained to tell Kluge about our preparations. He knew generally what his operations officer was up to, and covered him. The only limit on his tacit approval was imposed by his legendary intelligence and prudence— not for nothing had he been nicknamed Günther the Crafty. To this sixty-year-old Prussian imbued with tradition, assassinating Hitler while he was eating lunch seemed a little cowardly for German officers. He had another reservation as well: the German people would not understand the murder of a man still perceived as an energetic war leader and the last bulwark against humiliating defeat. Hence, when I asked him about the plan, the field marshal did not answer me; instead, he gestured with his chin as if to say, "Do it at your own risk . . . I won't denounce you."

On March 7, Hans von Dohnanyi, Hans Oster's assistant, came to the headquarters of Army Group Center. Coded signals had been set up with him to launch the coup d'état in the event of the assassination's success. On March 12, 1943, the day before the Führer was to visit, we learned that Heinrich Himmler, head of the SS, would not be coming along with him. Kluge withdrew his approval at the last minute: to kill Hitler without seizing Himmler was to risk starting a civil war. As soon as the Führer was dead, the SS would take power and begin a merciless repression. It would then be necessary to dislodge them in turn from supreme power. In short, Hitler's elimination, though possible, would not have the necessary strategic significance without the concomitant liquidation of Himmler, the Reichsführer SS. The operation was canceled, and we were overwhelmed by a feeling of disappointment equal to the length we had gone to mobilizing for the project.

Flying in from Vinnytsya, the Führer's plane, a Focke-Wulf Condor, landed at the aerodrome. The stairs were lowered, the door opened, and Hitler descended. Himmler, as reported, was not there. The day was unbearable. At every stage of the visit, we were mentally following the development of the scenario for which we had so long planned, timed, and prepared. Hitler and Kluge were meeting in the conference room; I can still see the

Führer's personal physician, Professor Theodor Morell, snoring in the waiting room, his mouth open, insolent and tranquil while we cooled our heels. During the lunch, we had to put up with Hitler's good humor; he was glad to be among real soldiers. The Führer had brought along his personal cook and the physician assigned to taste his food. Hunched over his plate, his elbows on the table, raising his head only to swallow a mouthful of wine, he was a despicable sight.

We obeyed Kluge's interdiction. But Tresckow and Schlabrendorff had planned something else. Such a fine opportunity could not be missed: Hitler was not to live to the end of the day. As a simple reserve officer, Schlabrendorff felt less bound by the obligation of obedience incumbent on the regular soldier. During lunch Tresckow had ascertained that his tablemate Colonel Heinz Brandt was going to be in the Führer's plane on the way back. On the pretext of surprising Helmut Stieff, Schlabrendorff gave Brandt two bottles of French cognac in a wooden case. Gifts of wine and spirits were common among military men, and the sentry for the plane was easily taken in by Schlabrendorff's ruse. It was in reality a case of explosives, whose preparation had cost me several nights' work. The detonator, which Schlabrendorff had activated, was set to go off in midflight, somewhere near Minsk.

Our stupefaction was boundless when we learned that evening that the Führer's plane had landed safely in

Rastenburg, in East Prussia, after an uneventful flight. For Fabian von Schlabrendorff, the news was still more ominous. However, it was not yet time for lamentations. We had to act quickly, but not so abruptly as to arouse suspicion; hence, we could not arrange to take a special flight. Instead, the next day at dawn, Schlabrendorff left in a regularly scheduled mail plane. Two hours later, he was at the aerodrome where the Führer had landed. Maintaining his sangfroid, he found Brandt, recovered his case of cognac, and exchanged real wine bottles for the explosives. On examination, it turned out that the detonator had malfunctioned, probably owing to the extremely low temperature in the plane's baggage compartment.

The following week, in Berlin, Gersdorff was supposed to show the Führer some of the spoils taken from the Soviets. He was to accompany General Walther Model. Tresckow had managed at the last minute to send this pro-Nazi general instead of Kluge, whom he wanted to be available in the event that the assassination attempt succeeded. March 20 was Heroes' Day, dedicated to the memory of the hundreds of thousands of soldiers who had already fallen at the front. Joseph Goebbels and Hermann Göring were also to be present: another unhoped-for opportunity. Gersdorff was supposed to sacrifice himself in this attempt. Our common desire to eliminate the Führer was such that Gersdorff hadn't hesitated for a moment when Tresckow suggested the idea to him. A few moments after the Führer entered the arsenal, he activated the time bomb attached to his belt. Unfortunately, Hitler was in a hurry, and passed through the exposition at a run, without listening to any of the explanations and without pausing before the display cases, despite Göring's urging. Left alone, Gersdorff had time to rush to the lavatory, smash the detonator, and flush it down the toilet. He had saved his own life, but Hitler was still alive.

These two failures, which occurred a week apart, were not enough to destroy our morale. We knew we could count on one another; that was what mattered. But looking back, I have to admit that Kluge was right. In March 1943, our conspiracy was not yet mature enough to succeed. The simple physical elimination of the Führer would have solved nothing without a well-planned coup d'état. We would only have paved the way for another despot, who might have been still more bloodthirsty. It was in fact highly unlikely that the elite anti-Nazi elements would agree to expose themselves in order to organize the immediate and coordinated reaction required.

15

Stopping the Barbarians

When the fighting on the eastern front began, German officers felt that they represented civilization in a battle against a barbarous nation. What is barbarism? First of all, it is a complete disrespect for the rights of individuals, brutality in human relations, savagery in the conduct of everyday life, and finally, indifference to all the attainments of culture and comfort, to everything of beauty that centuries of labor and the progress of the human spirit have produced. These Communists whose agents would not hesitate to shoot soldiers in retreat; these officers without conscience who sent hastily raised ragtag groups of women, old men, and children toward us to be mowed down by our machine guns just to exhaust German munitions; these enemies who systematically executed the wounded, put out the eyes of prisoners, and didn't deign even to bury their own dead—they all seemed barbarians to us. We had heard many stories, and we had seen many instances of macabre proof that they were true. But for months now we had also known that the Russians had no monopoly on barbarism: bestiality had taken hold of the SS and their auxiliaries, and even regular soldiers sometimes acted with senseless cruelty. And so we had not only to prevent the Russian steam-roller from crushing eastern Europe, but also to curb the SS's capacity for destruction. This conviction, at first vaguely felt, was quickly confirmed for me.

In the early spring of 1943, when I had just taken command of my battalion, Bettermann, who commanded the artillery group, asked to speak to me privately. He seemed very upset. For two days, on his way back from leave, he had traveled in the same railway car with SS men and men from the Sicherheitsdienst (SD) and had had to put up with their endless conversations. The SS men were loudly bragging about having liquidated, in Army Group South's sector, no less than two hundred fifty thousand Jews. Drunk on brandy, they took pleasure in recounting the massacres, mixing cruel and obscene details. Though he turned away in disgust, my artilleryman still heard that they were soon to move into Army Group Center's sector to ply their trade there.

I didn't hesitate for a second; I called Georg on the phone. "I have to see Kluge, immediately!"

"What's wrong?" Georg asked, astonished by my agitation.

"Major, I'll tell you later. Nothing to do with the regiment!"

"All right, go ahead," Georg said, hanging up; he had understood the gravity of the situation by my tone and the official address.

Less than an hour later, I was at headquarters. The marshal saw me immediately, and took what I said very seriously. "We absolutely have to prevent such a catastrophe. Go see Tresckow and take care of it."

True to his reputation, Tresckow provided the solution to a problem that appeared insoluble. It was impossible to prevent the SD from coming in, or to prevent its members from committing atrocities. The ground had to be cut out from under them; they had to be deprived of the means of conducting roundups. Tresckow therefore ordered all local commandants to prohibit any assembly of citizens within their areas. Without the ability to gather their victims together before putting them into the trucks, the SS would be seriously hindered. In fact, the SD's anti-Semitic atrocities were more limited in this zone than in others on the eastern front, and especially in the Ukraine. I was able to confirm this when visiting the Yad Vashem memorial in Jerusalem a few years ago.

16

Cavalrymen in Torment

During a lecture I, along with other members of the German and the French resistances, gave in Paris in January 2004 before a group of secondary school students, a young man asked me, "But why, after all, didn't you organize other conspiracies? Why didn't you try again and again?"

"It was wartime!" I replied. "Our primary role, as officers, was to make sure our men survived and returned home."

It seems to me important to repeat this point here. It is true that our objective was to eliminate the Führer and to overthrow the regime. We were doing our duty, fulfilling our ultimate obligation. But we also had an immediate operational assignment, a responsibility toward the men we commanded that could not be evaded. The eastern front took virtually all our energy, our concentration, and our physical and psychological capacities. The dates planned for assassination attempts were intertwined with the requirements of the operational calendar. That is why, the day before the Führer visited our headquarters in March 1943, Georg and his men had been far more absorbed in an engagement with guerrilla forces than with the material preparation for the assassination.

In May the cavalry group was still heavily involved in fighting with the partisans around Staiki, between Vitebsk and Orsha. During the retreat, it was one of the few units to remain mobile, while the trucks were floundering in the melting snow, their advance halted by streams that had turned into torrents. Then the regiment was given a supplementary battalion commanded by Captain Bassewitz. Fortunately, the operational necessities left us a few moments for relaxation. In June, for example, we organized an equestrian tournament and a Roman chariot race, with drivers wearing togas.

When we had nothing else to do, we performed intensive training exercises in dismounting to fight on foot (*Absitzen zum Kampf*). The horses had long since become accustomed to the din of gunfire, the sound of explosions, and the shouts of the combatants; they showed an amazing placidity. But they remained vulnerable to fire. In each battle, the cavalry had to be ready to dismount at short notice, leaving their animals without unsettling brusqueness and handing them over to one of their comrades who was assigned to take them a few hundred paces toward the rear. Each man responsible for this maneuver, who remained in the saddle, had to be able to hold the bridle of one horse in his right hand and the reins of two more in his left. He would depart at a trot, under the direction of an experienced adjutant, to wait out the fighting in the shelter of a forest or behind a hill. The little group of horses was then brought back to the combatants, sometimes guided by radio when the circumstances of the battle had forced the unit to move. These maneuvers had to be carried out in a few minutes at most. The quality of the training explains why the loss of mounts was minimal—so much so that in 1945, I was able to return home with Moritz and Oter, the horses that had been with me since 1939.

Soon, however, the fighting became more serious. On July 5, 1943, Hitler launched Operation Citadel, which was supposed to reduce or even annihilate the formidable offensive potential the enemy had assembled in the Kursk salient, an area between Army Group Center and Army Group South. The cavalry regiment was to play a decisive role. A visiting fireman, as Field Marshal Kluge wished it to be, the regiment's mission was to stay continually on the move putting out fires.

On July 12, 1943, eighty Soviet rifle divisions, supported by air cover and 3,500 tanks, counterattacked from the west and north Orel-Briansk panhandle, where large numbers of German troops had been concentrated

Operations briefing, Russia, July 1943.
Georg is in the middle; Philipp is at left.

for the attack on the Kursk salient, farther to the south. Two hundred kilometers southwest of Moscow, the Orel salient, an indentation penetrating into Russian territory, was symmetrical to the Kursk salient, which bulged into the positions held by the Wehrmacht.

Tresckow foresaw that we would be in danger of being surrounded if the Red Army succeeded in seizing the Orel-Karachev-Briansk railway line. He decided to send one of our battalions to the sector of Tereben, a large village northeast of Karachev. The infantry's ability to resist was exhausted there, and the line of defense was in the process of collapsing. Georg designated me for the operation. We put our six hundred men on a train camouflaged with whole birch trees, along with 62 light machine guns, 12 heavy machine guns, 1 antitank gun, and 1 antiaircraft gun.

Going ahead of our troops, Georg and I arrived at the command post in Tereben during the night of July 17. We found it in a state of total confusion. Two commandants were arguing over who was to take the initiative. Georg reconciled them by depriving both of any authority over their seven battalions. Then gunshots rang out north of the village. The troops, panicked, began running down the streets. Georg, his pistol in his hand, worked his way up the human stream, managing to turn the flow around and to rally the defenders. The men recovered their courage, but the adversary's numerical superiority was incontestable. To hold Tereben, we had to temporarily abandon the defense of the village of Kudrjavez, four kilometers to the southeast. The next day, however, Georg was ordered to retake this village. We had to catch the enemy by surprise. I left with my men at 8:00 a.m. on July 20, went around the village on the west side, continued a few kilometers farther south, and then, suddenly changing direction, headed north and penetrated enemy territory, destroying a Russian supply column on the way. Georg, who had taken up a position north of the village, guided our movements by radio. In two hours, the village had been retaken along with important booty, especially intelligence materials. Our casualties were three dead and twenty-one wounded. The respite was short.

At dawn on July 23, the enemy resumed the offensive. Seven Russian rifle regiments attacked the defense line, which had been hastily set up and was only lightly manned. Georg used his units as emergency reinforcements. When our infantrymen weakened at a point, he brought in one or two detachments of forty cavalrymen who dispersed the Russian infantry, reestablished the line, and then went to deal with another hot spot. The whole defense would no doubt have collapsed had it not been for Georg, who was fighting alongside his troops.

The Third Cavalry Squadron found itself in the worst difficulties. It had lost contact with the troops on its left and right. Reduced in half an hour to 110 men, it seemed doomed to be completely wiped out. Then Georg suddenly emerged from a thicket, accompanied by his driver.

Wearing his forage cap while bullets whistled around his ears and armed only with a pistol stuck into his belt and a stick in his hand, he went to join the head of the squadron. With total composure, he asked for a report on the situation, as if the drama playing out all around him were only a training maneuver. When the men saw him, his obvious assurance was enough to reinvigorate them. Like a teacher, Georg then asked, "All right, now, what would you do? Would you make a frontal attack? Or would you prefer to infiltrate laterally between the two enemy regiments?" The leader of the squadron opted for a frontal advance. Georg took a few moments to think: "Fine, stay here, and don't give up an inch of terrain; reestablish connection with the unit on your left, and I'll take care of the rest." Thirty minutes later, with the squadron placed under his direct command, he attacked the enemy regiment's flank, forcing a retreat. Georg immediately returned to the Third Squadron and ordered it to resume an all-out offensive in coordination with the lateral attack. The operation worked perfectly. The Russians were driven back. But we had gained only a few hours, because the enemy's firepower was over-whelming. Soon Tereben was in flames. Our three battalions were much diminished. Two battalions were still more or less able to fight, but exhausted by the incessant battles of the preceding days, they would not hold out for long. The cavalry, which was still operational, saw the number of its able-bodied men cut in half.

By 4:00 p.m. on July 24, we had to face facts and give up Tereben and Kudrjavez. The new objective was the bridge over the Resseta, a little to the west. At the risk of cutting off their own retreat, Georg's men blew up the bridge at 6:00 p.m. The remaining troops were supposed to move about fifteen kilometers to the southwest along the river, while at the same time protecting the rail line; the Russians pursuing them were threatening to pass them by on the left flank. Between the adversary and the German units there was a marshy area. Here and there little thickets grew on the spongy soil. The rest was a broad marsh, sometimes a meter deep, infested with mosquitoes and leeches. On July 27 we were ordered to attack. In two hours of fierce but prudent fighting, we routed an enemy battalion, capturing dozens of Russian soldiers caught in the watery trap.

By July 29 the situation had been stabilized. We were relieved by two neighboring divisions. Georg and I remained in reserve in the sector until August 8. These two weeks of intense fighting had resulted in a limited number of losses to our unit: 7 percent dead, 29 percent wounded.

During the summer our regiment's various battalions were successively mobilized for duty in several hot spots around Smolensk. The scenario was always the same: the enemy's numerical superiority; penetrations that sowed panic in our ranks; the rapid intervention of the cavalry, which created a temporary stability; the evacuation of what could be evacuated; and then, under assault by further waves of attackers, an orderly retreat of our units. The cavalrymen, in short, provided an orderly management of the inevitable retreat.

In mid-September, Kluge succeeded in convincing Hitler to abandon Smolensk. Army Group Center retreated on a part of the front called the Panther Line, which stretched from Vitebsk in the north to Gomel in the south. On September 25 the marshal ordered Georg to concentrate his troops southeast of Orsha; they were to be put at the disposition of the Fourth Army. Our regiment covered the 126 kilometers in thirty-six hours and reached the point indicated on September 27 at 8:00 a.m. We had to go immediately on the attack. For the first time, we took as part of our booty American radio equipment, tangible proof of deliveries from the United States to their Soviet ally. In early October, its mission accomplished, the regiment moved back to the north, under torrential rains.

But the regiment had to prepare itself for graver ordeals. Toward mid-October, the Russians broke the Panther Line at several points. Anticipating that such a break might take place, the line had been backed up first by the East Panther Line and then by the West Panther Line, separated by a few kilometers. One day, a reconnaissance patrol that I had sent into this unsecured area came under enemy fire. It took refuge in a forest and wandered about for a whole day in the marshy under-

growth, the horses sinking in up to their bellies. Sandbanks with pines on them emerged here and there from
the watery expanse. The patrol bivouacked on one of
these sandbanks, curled up on a few square meters like a
hedgehog in a defensive position. The men ended up giving their bread ration to the exhausted horses, for whom
the birch branches they were offered were not enough.
The next day, evading the enemy, the patrol managed to
rejoin the battalion. How relieved I was to see these boys
that I thought were lost! I handed out cognac liberally
and gave each man twenty cigarettes—a luxury in those
times.

Georg soon decided to use the battalion I commanded, because the Second Battalion had been over-
worked in the preceding weeks. My unit's strength had
already been sharply diminished; I had only one-third of
my normal number of machine guns. So it was with 19
light machine guns, 4 heavy machine guns, and 7 grenade
launchers that we took up, on October 21, our position in
Sapolje. The mission was simple but suicidal: we were to
retake the part of the old East Panther Line that the Soviets had held comfortably for several days.

Georg went out alone at dawn to examine the terrain. He saw that the enemy, overwhelming two infantry
companies, had made a breakthrough. Quickly marshal-
ing two cavalry detachments on reconnaissance that he
had happened to run into, he launched, in his own way,
an improvised counterattack. The little group (fewer

than seventy cavalrymen) headed toward the Russians at a gallop. The soldiers then noticed with terror that Georg was not armed. They offered him a pistol, but he laughed and rode on. When the Russians came into view, Georg separated his troops into two detachments, which attacked the enemy on both flanks. Taken by surprise, the Russians were routed in a few minutes, leaving behind them forty prisoners and as many dead. Without delay, our men galloped off to the regiment's operations command post.

The next day, my men retook the village of Redki without a fight. Then we were ordered to take a rise somewhat to the south of the village, known as Hill 208. We approached it without difficulty. But we still had to cross a natural glacis—two hundred meters of open slope leading to the summit. In briefing the troops, I had been clear: "The quicker we carry out the assault, the fewer our losses." I was not wrong. Mortar shells fell all around us. We had to launch several attacks in order to take the hill, with considerable losses, and ended up fighting hand to hand. We achieved our objective in the afternoon, but we already had thirty-two dead, nearly 10 percent of our troops. And we still hadn't won, because less than a kilometer away the Russian artillery, positioned on another hill, was able to shell the one we had taken with such difficulty. The Russians' aim was accurate: a whole group of my men was cut down, or rather pulverized, as soon as they took up positions on the summit. We worked all night, restoring the trenches and resupplying the 400-square-meter area at the foot of the hill that separated the battalion from the next division. We also took advantage of the darkness to evacuate the dead and wounded, who had been loaded onto small carts.

At dawn the Russians attacked. They had crept up to the foot of the hill, taking cover in the small bushes and depressions in the terrain. They were thrown back twice. Here the cavalrymen were fighting like infantry in trench warfare, using rifles and machine guns. Soon the Russian artillery resumed its intensive bombardment, concentrating its firepower on the summit of the hill. The exploding shells shredded the thin layer of grass on the hilltop, uncovering sandy, shifting soil. Dust blew in everywhere, jamming the last machine guns that had not been put out of commission by the Soviet artillery. I was wounded, but still remained on the battlefield for some time. By ten o'clock, weak and dizzy with pain, I had to be evacuated. By eleven-thirty, the situation had become critical. The hill could no longer be held. Our losses were too great, and the attacks were unrelenting. Several of the battalion's units had suffered 95 percent casualties, killed or wounded. The operational forces thrown into battle by the regimental commandant had been reduced to 120 men. At nightfall, the few dozen remaining able-bodied men were preparing to abandon the hill when Russian patrols attacked the lines, broke through the defenses, and began to surround our troops. Pursuers and pursued mixed in the same chaotic race. Our men retreated as best they could toward the operations command post that had been set up in the village.

Georg was inside the command post. His second in command, Lieutenant Gigas, was struggling to establish a telephone connection with the divisional command. "Major," he said, "something is wrong on the main highway and Hill 208, there's heavy fire and it's getting closer."

Georg didn't realize how great the threat was until Dr. Keltsch, the First Battalion's physician, suddenly burst into the shack. "The Russians are here," he cried breathlessly. Georg hurried outside and saw about sixty exhausted men grouped around the few armored vehicles he had at his disposal in the Redki sector. Three tanks were quickly rounded up, along with two antiaircraft guns. They were firing blindly into the dark. The Russians were coming down the slopes of the hill in successive waves and falling upon the remains of the battalion, protected by the darkness.

"Alert the engineering troops in Ssudilovitch," Georg shouted to Lieutenant Gigas before collapsing; he had been hit by an enemy bullet. The staff's physician, Dr. Deecke, saw that Georg had a deep wound in his hip. My brother was evacuated. Gigas, whom Georg had put in command, had great difficulty in evacuating the men toward the West Panther Line. On the way, the group, already small, was attacked again, leaving behind still more dead, and once more were overwhelmed by panic. The lieutenant managed to reestablish order in the ranks by pointing out that they were crossing a minefield with only a very narrow path that was safe.

At last they reached the longed-for German lines. The men collapsed with fatigue. Though in retreat, Lieutenant Gigas had retained his ability to make decisions. He sent a handful of soldiers back to Redki, where the Russians were celebrating their rout of the Germans with heavy drinking. Without being noticed, the patrol managed to slip into the little house that had served as a command post. There it recovered maps, intelligence materials, and Georg's precious fur-lined coat before returning safely to our lines.

On October 28 the remains of the regiment were withdrawn from the Panther Line and left the Fourth Army. For two months the regiment rebuilt its strength, trained recruits, transformed hundreds of infantrymen into cavalrymen, and incorporated new officers.

Georg and I, who had been wounded a few hours apart, were both taken to the military hospital in Minsk, where we were soon joined by Marshal Kluge. Seriously injured in an automobile accident—partisans had thrown a milk can at his windshield—he had given up command of Army Group Center. Less than a month later, I was able to resume command of my battalion. Georg's wound, which was more of a problem, confined him to desk work until the end of December. He continued to direct operations from a distance. He went to great lengths to obtain authorization to equip his men with MP-43 submachine guns, which were very easy to handle and well adapted to the Russian context. In pursuing this project he was opposing the views of Hitler's circle, which feared that too much diversification of armaments would have deleterious effects on production lines. He finally got what he wanted; the Ministry of Armament surreptitiously encouraged experimentation with new equipment, and almost two thousand of the MP-43s were delivered in early 1944.

Despite the soldiers' bravery, the sacrifice of whole units, and the technical quality of the command, the Wehrmacht could no longer stand up to an enemy that was constantly growing in numbers and equipment. According to Kluge's analysis, Army Group Center needed more than two hundred thousand additional men. Each division had to hold a sector twenty to thirty kilometers wide, and the front lines had become too porous to allow the cavalry to fill the gaps. The eastern front was disintegrating.

17

The Valise Full of Explosives

In the early autumn of 1943, Georg ordered me to take some explosives to Stieff, now a general. In concert with Tresckow, then on leave in Berlin, he had started looking again for practical ways to carry out Operation Valkyrie, from a bomb attack to a coup d'état. It was no longer a question of an isolated assassination, but rather of beginning a complete overthrow of the regime.

As the regiment's bomb expert, I had access to explosives in reasonable quantities, and had no difficulty removing some from our stocks. I took a regularly scheduled flight to the army headquarters in the Mauerwald camp near Lötzen, fifteen kilometers from the Führer's Wolfsschanze. In my leather valise I carried explosives and detonators. The explosives were in the form of twenty bricks sheathed in aluminum.

The Valise Full of Explosives

The lingering effects of my wounds left me with a limp, and it was therefore agreed that a car would be waiting to take me to Stieff. When I got to the aerodrome, however, there was no one there, and so I tried to limp along carrying my heavy load. I had to ward off a zealous NCO who was passing through and offered to help. Finally, the car turned up and took me to Helmut Stieff. The general was in a conference, and I had to wait. Impatient, nervous, and clinging to my valise, I slipped into the staff's movie theater, which was open day and night. The darkness provided a little tranquility, but I couldn't pay the slightest bit of attention to the comedy that was being shown—*Das Bad auf der Tenne*. Spectators were coming and going as they went on and off duty. I gripped my valise with both hands, holding it between my legs and taking care that no one tripped over it. Finally someone came to get me. Stieff had left word not to be disturbed for any reason, and we locked ourselves into a windowless archive room. In a few minutes I handed over the explosives, explained how to use them, took my leave, and returned by the same route.

It was only after the war that I found out what happened to my valise. In November, Stieff went on leave and entrusted the explosives to Herwarth von Bitterfeld,[1] second in command to General Köstring, who was in charge of the troops on the eastern front. At that time, Herwarth and his boss lived in a barracks called the *Jägerhöhe*, near army headquarters. They had facing rooms on the same hallway. German women from the Banat region cleaned the rooms every other day, doing one side of the hallway one day and then the other side the next. Herwarth had hidden the precious valise under his bed. When his room was to be cleaned, he slipped it under the general's bed, across the hall, and retrieved it that evening. He'd told Köstring what Stieff had told him: "Don't look in the valise, its contents are too hot for you!" Thus, for several months, the valise traveled back and forth between the two rooms.

In the early summer of 1944, Stieff recovered the valise and gave it to Colonel Claus von Stauffenberg.[2] What happened next is well known.

18

Obligatory Inactivity

From November 1943 to March 1944, Georg and I spent more time in military hospitals than on the battlefield. My brother's condition continued to deteriorate. He had returned to his troops shortly before Christmas 1943. But his immune system had been weakened by overwork, and he really needed to remain completely inactive. At the end of December, he began to run a high fever and was moved from Kolodichi to Minsk. On examining his wounds, the military doctors discovered that he had developed multiple infections and was at risk of developing septicemia. Georg was therefore condemned to another period of rest.

During this time, our regiment, along with its 900 horses, 20 trucks, 5 tanks, and many light machine guns, was transferred to the Petrikov sector on the Pripyat

With Lieutenant Schulte (right) at Patrykozy (fifteen kilometers north of Second Army headquarters at Petrikov), 1944.

River, where the Second Army's staff, which Tresckow had headed since November, was located. Tresckow had two main concerns. First, he wanted to keep "his" cavalry regiment near him: Operation Valkyrie was now set, and he had to be ready to act at any moment. Second, he needed to secure the eighty to one hundred kilometers separating him from Army Group South. To be sure, the Rokitno marshes, whose waters did not freeze, formed a kind of natural defense, but they were not impenetrable. Tresckow had at first envisaged making sporadic use of the regiment for impromptu commando actions. But the situation, which had suddenly deteriorated, forced him to accelerate the transfer of the regiment and to mobilize my battalion immediately.

We covered the 250 kilometers by train. On the night of December 31, 1943, the train stopped in the snow. Not a sound, no one around, no lights—just an icy wind, blowing through the forest powdered with frost. It was 11:30 p.m. The closest German defense posts were more than six kilometers away, and the men were concerned that there might be a mechanical problem. But soon my order was passed from one car to another: all batteries were to be set up to test the cannons. At least, that was the official reason—my boys needed comforting, and this huge fireworks show (as many as twenty-five cannon shots) would please my cavalrymen and dissuade Russian partisans from attacking our convoy. The sector we were entering was desolate. In the tireless struggle against the partisans infesting the region, the SS had devastated, massacred, and burned down whole villages. Only a few inhabitants were still holed up in cellars.

On January 9, 1944, the battalion was assigned to repel a Russian breakthrough. The squadron commanded by Lieutenant Hidding, which had been sent to the site and entrenched, was supposed to resist, with only 60 men, three squadrons of enemy cavalry equipped with a number of light machine guns and an antitank battery. Russian losses were dreadful but, subjected to a storm of artillery fire, our forces were soon reduced to about 40 individuals. Then I arrived with the two other squadrons. Our counterattack succeeded in less than three-quarters of an hour, thanks to the effectiveness of the machine pistols we had just received. The next day, the fighting favored us less. On the evening of January 10, I radioed Kolodichi to request 150 men to replace those I had lost over the preceding two days. In the Third Cavalry Squadron alone, there were 44 dead. I was wounded again, for the fifth time since the beginning of the war. On January 11, a plane sent by Tresckow evacuated me to the military hospital in Minsk.

Georg's health and my own became so much a matter of concern that the high command got involved. Georg, whose doctors couldn't keep him in bed, had started riding again too soon. His wounds had reopened, and the loss of blood nearly killed him. At the suggestion of Field Marshal Ernst von Busch, the new commander in chief of Army Group Center, we were both transferred to a hospital in Germany. Then began two long months of inactivity, in the hands of calm and vigilant nuns, in a fairy-tale town, in the shadow of the monastery's bronze bell tower. Münstereifel was only a few dozen kilometers away from Heimerzheim. In that little town, which was hardly threatened by air raids, we felt at home; we received visits from our friends and relatives, and the war seemed infinitely far away.

I was able to resume my command in March 1944, after having handed it over for two months to Wilhelm König. Georg remained on bed rest until Easter 1944. Two weeks later, still not fully recovered, he set out for Russia. At only twenty-eight years of age, he had to use a cane to walk, and was emaciated. When he reached the front on April 25, he went back to work with all his old vigor. In his absence, important details had been neglected, and errors had been committed. He dismissed three officers the day after he returned. Although he had been promoted to lieutenant colonel the preceding December, he was no longer the sole master of his unit. Since February, the Thirty-first Cavalry Regiment had been integrated into a cavalry brigade. It had been decided not to offer the command of the new brigade to Georg, who was not yet thirty, but rather to an experienced cavalryman of forty-one, Baron von Wolff, who was of Baltic origin. The Third Cavalry Brigade (two other brigades were constituted at the same time, one in the north and one in the south) was in reality scarcely any stronger than Georg's old regiment. Each brigade had been reduced from three to two regiments, and each regiment from three to two battalions, so that Wolff commanded only four battalions.

19

The Dangerous Ride

JULY 1944

In early June 1944 the Russian front seemed for a time to have been stabilized; it was the calm before the storm. But the situation of the Third Cavalry Brigade was hardly enviable. With fewer than three thousand men, it was supposed to defend fifty-five kilometers of the front and guard eighteen bridges; it took the supply column ten hours to make its daily deliveries. The administration was deficient, certain specialities were no longer represented, the men were not always well trained, and, crucially, by the end of the fifth year of war, equipment delivered to us was sometimes unusable—like the three hundred saddles we received without girths. The invasion of Normandy exacerbated a situation already extremely unfavorable to Germany. On June 12, after the Allies had landed 326,000 soldiers on the coast of France, it was

clear that a breakthrough on the eastern front was imminent. On June 22 the Soviets launched a gigantic frontal
attack against Army Group Center; no fewer than 2.5
million men advanced on one-sixth as many German
troops.

On June 26, with the situation extremely critical,
Georg went on leave. Why did he, known for his devotion and his acute sense of responsibility to his men, leave
the front at a time like that? Faced with the magnitude of
the task, had he become discouraged? No. For the past
eighteen months, Georg had known that collapse was
imminent, and he sought only to delay it with the mini-
mum of losses. For the moment, he wanted to devote all
his energy to a maneuver Tresckow had asked him to
carry out. After spending a few hours at Heimerzheim,
he said farewell to our family, perhaps with a premoni-
tion that he would never see them again. Then he went
to Paris on the fatuous pretext, still taken seriously despite
the gravity of the military situation, that Lord Wagram (a
stallion of ours, which would be confiscated by the
French a few months later) was running at Longchamp!

In Paris, at 8:00 p.m. on July 3, Field Marshal Kluge
took command of the western front. As soon as he
arrived, Georg was received by the marshal. He set forth
Tresckow's proposal: first, to eliminate Hitler; second,
not to oppose the Allies' breakthrough but to surrender
unconditionally on the western front, and then to shift
the war effort entirely to Russia to prevent Germany

from being crushed by the Soviet war machine; third, to make a peace offer to the Allies, for which purpose Georg agreed to go to England. Kluge sharply rejected this proposal on every point, irritated by what he considered Tresckow's irresponsible conduct: "It is pointless to offer the Allies points of entry, because their breakthrough is imminent, and the collapse of the western front is now only days away!" It was pointless as well, he added, to think about going to England: he couldn't find a pilot reliable enough to carry out such a delicate operation while fighting raged on the shores of the English Channel. Sick at heart, Georg returned to Russia.

In the East, our marshals had a single concern: to simplify the front line. The bulges and indentations had to be removed to facilitate defense and make up for the shortage of men, which was becoming more and more manifest. The front had to run along straight lines in order to gain hundreds of kilometers and delay the enemy's implacable advance. Hitler had decided, against all strategic requirements, that the existing positions had to be held at any cost. He declared several particularly exposed cities to be "fixed strongpoints." In a few days the Russians swept the front away and pulverized the so-called strongpoints. In less than three weeks, the German army lost 350,000 men on the Russian front. Within Army Group Center, the Fourth and Ninth armies were annihilated, and the Third Panzer Army was scattered in all directions. Of my brother Georg's old Sixth Infantry

Division, there remained but a few remnants. Only the Second Army, with ten divisions and one cavalry corps, remained more or less intact, but it was still vulnerable. At its head, Tresckow, still assisted by Schlabrendorff, had succeeded in stopping the enemy and defending his positions. But the cavalry brigade was particularly exposed and frequently called upon, for it was ideally suited to covering a retreat. Georg could have asked to command it, because know-how was needed. Baron von Wolff had been killed during an exercise on June 28, and my brother's claim to the position was all the stronger because Field Marshal Busch was arguing for his appointment. But he now had other priorities. He therefore voluntarily remained on the staff, at Tresckow's disposal. The last act of the conspiracy was at hand.

It was in this context that the gamble of July 20, 1944, took place. On July 1 the appointment of Lieutenant Colonel Claus von Stauffenberg as chief of staff of the Reserve Army gave him access to the Führer. None of the conspirators had ever before been able to get so close to the target. On July 11, Stauffenberg made a first attempt by bringing a bomb into the Berghof, Hitler's residence in Berchtesgaden. The absence of Himmler and Göring, however, led him to abort the attempt, though in Berlin his accomplice, General Friedrick Olbricht, had already launched Operation Valkyrie. Not without difficulty, this operation was stopped, and the first steps toward a coup d'état and the mobilization of troops stationed in Germany were disguised as a simple exercise. On July 15 Stauffenberg tried again—and again stopped short, for the same reasons. He would have only one more chance; if he failed again, Operation Valkyrie would inevitably be compromised.

At the beginning of July, I went to Second Army headquarters to say hello to Tresckow. As he saw me off, he warned, "Take care of yourself! We are soon going to need your services!" Georg and I realized that the assassination attempt was about to be made. We knew our roles by heart, but we didn't know exactly what the others were to do. We weren't told what part Stauffenberg would play, or precisely how the assassination in the Führer's headquarters would take place. This was perfectly normal; to be effective, a conspiracy has to remain compartmentalized.

Georg had assigned me to be ready to discreetly withdraw the equivalent of six squadrons (about 1,200 men) from the front. The goal was to transfer them to Berlin just after the assassination, in order to provide security in particularly sensitive parts of the capital. On July 14 or 15 Georg confirmed these instructions. It was not, properly speaking, an order, because at headquarters he did not have authority over the Thirty-first Cavalry Regiment, and still less over the brigade. That was what made my situation uncomfortable. I had to act on my own initiative, without formal instructions. Obviously, I would be covered by Tresckow if asked to explain what I was doing, but it was up to me to determine the exact modalities for the retreat and the transfer of troops. The operational situation of the Second Army, which was threatened on all sides, was totally unpredictable. Therefore I had to improvise and work against the clock. Providing 1,200 men was not an easy task!

On July 6 the Second Army's Twentieth Corps had been ordered to retreat. The cavalry brigade, aided by a few Hungarian hussars, was supposed to cover the withdrawal of parts of the infantry. From July 11 on, my regiment was constantly engaged with the enemy north of the two ground links—the road and the rail line— between Pinsk, which had just been evacuated, and Brest-Litovsk. Georg followed these operations with extreme vigilance; he was obsessed with preventing his cavalrymen from being caught in a trap. At 4:00 a.m. on July 16 my regiment arrived in Dohoty, after having ridden half the night. At 8:00 a.m. Dohoty was attacked again by Russian forces much superior in numbers to ours. Soviet fighter planes constantly streaked across the sky, while we had no air cover at all. It was no longer a question of whether we should retreat, but how. The next day, this catastrophic scenario began all over again.

On July 15 I had taken the precaution of withdrawing a squadron of two hundred men from the front. They had already started for Berlin. I told the brigade's second in command about the withdrawal of these men from combat, and later had great difficulty in explaining their

The Dangerous Ride

reappearance—which was necessary, however, in order to acquire sufficient provisions. I claimed that I had written one too many zeroes . . . for although twenty soldiers can easily appear or disappear, the same does not go for a whole squadron.

I then requisitioned the five additional squadrons we had in mind for Operation Valkyrie and assembled them in the morning, near Rybno, eight kilometers southeast of the town of Kobryn. These were three of the four squadrons under my command, and two of Captain Gollert-Hansen's. On July 18, after giving the units a short rest, we distributed munitions and food supplies for two days, and set out. The officers were very surprised, for these marching orders canceled others received only hours earlier.

The administrative officer of the Third Cavalry Brigade, Lieutenant Gigas, saw to it that Army Group Center put forty large-capacity trucks at our disposal. Gigas knew enough about the plot to realize that this directive had to be carried out perfectly, but he did not know about the assassination itself. The trucks were to assemble at Konopka. From there they would carry about one thousand men, piled under tarps, toward an aerodrome in the former Poland. Then they would immediately fly to Berlin's Tempelhof Airport. Finally, they would go to Prinz-Albert-Strasse and Wilhelmstrasse, where they would take control of the buildings occupied by the state security police and the Ministry of

Propaganda. But first of all, they had to ride on horseback the two hundred kilometers from Rybno to Konopka.

How, with the war in full swing, could one carry out a maneuver of this kind without arousing suspicion? How could the withdrawal of so many troops go unnoticed? The fact was that the disintegration of the front was so advanced that battalions and even squadrons were attached to their brigades and to their divisions only with regard to logistics and supply. From an operational point of view, the basic units, which were supposed to constitute a self-sufficient point of resistance to the enemy's advance, were put under the control of an army corps commander. This abbreviated chain of command short-circuited all the intermediate levels. Moreover, in the chaotic retreat, squadrons, detachments, and even patrols were largely autonomous. The movements of the cavalry-men thus took place without either the brigade comman-der or the regimental commander being informed. They were all the less surprised by this momentary disappear-ance, because it had been planned to withdraw the cavalry from the front to Brest-Litovsk and to hold it in reserve.

Furthermore, the cavalry's tactics of defense and retreat provided us with good cover. The retreat, in fact, took place through the successive movements of three lines. The first line (A–C) was supposed to reconnoiter, sometimes far behind the front, and to purge the sector of partisans. It began setting up a retreat position (digging trenches, camouflaging artillery pieces, cutting down pine trees to make fortifications, running barbed wire, and so on). A second line (D–E), about three to five kilometers behind the front, laid mines, drew up a chart of them, and prepared to blow up bridges and roads at the most critical points. The third line (F–G) was the only one engaged in defensive combat. When it had to retreat, the second line of defense, well installed in its entrenched positions, could in turn resist the enemy assault. The troops withdrawn from the front then established a new line A–C, and so on. Thus, it was usual to see units leaving the combat zone and galloping a few kilometers toward the rear.

The remnants of the Thirty-first Cavalry Regiment covered the infantry's retreat. When the latter had established a new line of defense, I withdrew all my cavalrymen from the front. At my last operations command post, I had received a green light from Georg: "To Berlin!" I took the car and during the night caught up with the squadrons on their way to Brest-Litovsk. The cavalrymen continued on their way for a day and a night without dismounting. Some of them, beyond exhaustion, fell asleep in the saddle and slipped to the ground. The lingering effects of my wounds prevented me from riding for hours on end. Therefore, I sometimes directed the movement of the three squadrons, and sometimes reconnoitered by automobile. Georg joined us and took command of the three squadrons. Brest-Litovsk had been designated as a fixed strongpoint. We had great difficulty in traversing the city without being requisitioned like every other unit that turned up there. Georg informed me by radio that he had managed to overcome the obstacles put in his way by the commandant of the place, and I was able to take my troops around the city on the north side. My brother then returned to be with Tresckow.

Apart from Georg and me, only two officers had been told about the ultimate goal of our maneuver: König—who had already been involved in the failed attempt of March 1943—and the head of the Third Squadron, Captain Hidding. The others who participated in this exhausting ride learned the secret only after the war. One detail of the operation, however, had surprised people: I had myself given the order to keep the horses at a trot when crossing cities. For a horseman, trotting on pavement is heresy, because the horse's shoes slip and put both rider and mount in danger. A few officers thus suspected something unusual, but they kept quiet about it. As the cavalrymen were crossing Brest-Litovsk, they rounded a corner and came face-to-face with Georg. They expected to be scolded, but he just shouted at them, "Faster, faster!" The men thought something very special must be going on.

We finally reached the village of Lachovka at 3:00 p.m. on July 20. I gave orders for the units to be reorganized and loaded on the trucks. The horses were to stay put, under guard of a few dozen men. In combat situations, the ratio was normally four horses per guard; this time it was ten per guard—another indication, for the most observant, that this was an exceptional operation.

While I was resting for a few moments in the shade of a birch tree, I was surprised to see my brother's regimental postmaster approach. Sergeant Retel was a dedicated Communist, but the whole regiment liked him. He handed me a paper on which Georg had scribbled this message: "Everyone to the old foxholes!" This was a code that meant that the assassination had not been carried out.

There was not a moment to lose. We immediately got back in the saddle and set out in the opposite direction, at the same breakneck speed, toward the front line, which had moved closer to us in the interim. It was only that evening that we heard on the radio about the failure of the assassination attempt and the catastrophe of the unsuccessful coup d'état. In the glum silence punctuated by the *clip-clop* of the horses' hooves, I had plenty of time for reflection. I was obsessed by one question: was it still really necessary to carry out this assassination? Stauffenberg had asked the same question of Tresckow a few days before the attempt. Why should one risk one's life, and especially that of dozens of other people, when the military situation suggested that in a few months the dictatorship would be over? Tresckow responded forthrightly, as usual: "The assassination has to take place, whatever the cost. Even if it doesn't succeed, we have to try. Now it is no longer the object of the assassination that matters, but rather to show the whole world, and history, that the German resistance movement dared to gamble everything, even at the risk of its own life. All the rest, in the end, is merely secondary."

I took a dim view of my future. The connection between the ride of the 1,200 and the conspiracy that had been discovered was much too obvious not to put Georg and me in danger. Soon I would be asked to account for what I'd done, and it would be very difficult to explain our four hundred kilometer ride, especially since it had not been without losses. During the night of July 19, in fact, I had stopped my car along the road a little to the northwest of Brest-Litovsk: I was watching the cavalry units file by, monitoring the condition of the animals and the men. Then I heard in the distance the sound of a mine exploding. Generally speaking, the explosion of a mine, whose force is largely absorbed by the belly of the mount, killed the horse but only wounded the rider's legs. This time, Captain Hidding had been killed instantly. Oddly, his squadron brought up the end of the column; a thousand men had passed over the same place before him. I raced back along the column. I had to inspect the victim's body as soon as possible, not only because he was a friend, but especially because he carried the maps of Berlin on which were marked in red pencil the areas that we were to seize, the itinerary from Tempelhof, and so on. These bits of evidence could not be allowed to fall into anyone else's hands. The body would be searched, because it was usual to send personal effects and valuables (medals, watches, wedding rings, signet rings, and so on) to the next of kin. Hidding was lying by the wayside; I approached the body and was able to keep others away on the pretext that I wanted to pray. Hunched over the cadaver, almost in contact with his disfigured face, I slipped my hand into his map bag, which was sticky with sweat and blood. I was able to extract the documents, which I hastily stuck inside my shirt. Then I allowed Hidding's orderly to proceed as usual in such cases. I had his coffin loaded onto a truck, with the hope of taking it back to Germany.[1]

At the same time another incident cost us still more dearly. As well as the forty trucks promised by Army Group Center, Captain Gigas had provided fifteen additional trucks, with thirty drivers and thirty men to accompany them. But near Brest-Litovsk, the military police diverted the convoy and made it go around the city on the north side. Unfortunately, it was ambushed by Russian tanks and cavalrymen, who had succeeded in making a breakthrough without the Germans' knowledge. Fourteen trucks and about fifty men were captured. One of the trucks managed to get away and was eventually abandoned, the men scattering in the surrounding wheat fields. One soldier thought he'd found a way to save himself by jumping onto a freight train that was passing nearby. But he quickly realized that the train, which was not under control—one of the engineers had been killed, the other wounded—was rolling toward a burning station where a Soviet tank would end up firing on them. The clandestine passenger jumped off the train and managed to get back to the German positions by passing through the fields.

The panic that reigned over the front was such that no one had really noticed the temporary disappearance of the various squadrons. During the rout, units often lost contact with one another. Sometimes an entire battalion was surrounded and destroyed. The high command was very happy to see 1,200 men appear—they constituted, after all, about 10 percent of the brigade's troops.

This was no time for explanations. Officers could not be harassed when maximum operational effectiveness was being asked of them. Therefore, Major Brinckmann, who commanded the regiment, did not ask me any questions.

20

A Time for Mourning

Shortly after the failed assassination attempt on July 20, 1944, Georg was named commander of the Third Cavalry Brigade. The responsibilities that awaited him were crushing and left no time for gloomy thoughts. In theory, he had under his command 11,500 men, the same number of horses, and a thousand Cossack cavalrymen as auxiliaries. In reality, he lacked more than 2,200 men, 200 auxiliaries, and about one-third of the planned equipment.

The battle raged all through the month of August. One incident almost cost Georg his life when he arrived at his new post. He had gone out early in the morning with his driver, who had defected from the Red Army. The road from the Second Army's headquarters to the brigade was considered secure, but their car was ambushed by the Russians. The two men immediately abandoned their vehicle, crossed a little prairie under fire, and took refuge in the undergrowth. Georg saw a murky pond covered with dead leaves and plant debris, in which the roots of several large trees formed natural hiding places. He and his reluctant driver entered the muddy water up to their chins and stayed there motionless. Beating the thickets with the butts of their rifles, firing pointblank into copses, the Russians searched for them in vain. Later in the morning, they came back with dogs, which were unable to track the two men in the malodorous swamp. The afternoon came, and everything seemed calm; birds were warbling. The driver started to move out of the water, but Georg held him back. As an experienced hunter, he had noticed that the birdsong was being imitated with bird whistles. They had to wait until the Russians got tired, gave up their search, and left the area at nightfall. Georg wanted at all costs to avoid falling into their hands. In the context of the period after July 20, his disappearance and capture by the enemy would have caused him to be seen as a traitor, and it would have directed the authorities' attention toward me, with questions regarding the true nature of our westward-bound ride. Major Kuhn, the operations officer for the Twenty-eighth Hussars Division, who also participated in the conspiracy and was also engaged to a member of Stauffenberg's family, had gone over to the enemy as soon as the failure of the assassination attempt became known.

*The two brothers with their comrades from
the Third Cavalry Brigade.*

His desertion was interpreted as a simple capture,[1] but a second case would have revealed this disguised escape for what it was.

The following weeks were depressing. The disintegration of the front continued as the beautiful, sunny summer wore on. One piece of terrible news after another reached me in the course of conversations. First Eberhard von Breitenbuch told me that Tresckow had died, immediately after the failure of the assassination attempt. Breitenbuch was the liaison officer for General Model, who had been made commandant of Army Group Center a few weeks earlier. On the morning of July 21, a car with a driver was posted in front of the Ostrow barracks, the seat of the Second Army command. Breitenbuch stood near the vehicle, waiting for Tresckow. In his earlier duty he had known Tresckow well, and he wanted to say good-bye to him. When Tresckow appeared, he was calm, relaxed, completely imbued with that inner balance that shaped his appearance. The sunshine seemed to herald a beautiful day—perhaps a little warm. Tresckow smiled at Breitenbuch. The young captain, who had heard about the failed assassination attempt very late the preceding night, excused himself for not being able to accompany his superior officer to the front, where the Twenty-eighth Rifle Regiment was located, because he had an assignment to carry out for General Model. He saw a flash of disappointment in Tresckow's eyes: "Too bad. I would have liked you to witness my death."

Tresckow, Georg, and Oertzen. All three died in the summer of 1944.

"But you're not going to . . ."

"Yes, I am. I don't want to let our enemies have the satisfaction of taking my life as well."

He had prepared everything: the pretense of an enemy ambush, the submachine gun he would be holding, the grenade that he would press against his belly. Tresckow told the distraught Breitenbuch what he wanted to happen afterward. Then, still as tranquil, he shook his hand firmly and said, "Good-bye. We will see each other in a better world." Tresckow got into the car, which then drove away, taking to his death the soul of this vast conspiracy in which Oster had been the brain, Beck the spinal marrow, and Stauffenberg the arm bearing the weapon. On July 21 Tresckow had sent his wife a farewell letter disguised as an ordinary note.[2] A few days earlier, he had sent his cherished Erika a newspaper clipping of this poem:

> A man who can keep his childhood dreams in all
>   their purity,
> Preserving them in his naked and defenseless
>   breast,
> Who, despite the laughter of this world, dares to
>   live as he had dreamed in his childhood,
> Down to his last day: yes, that is a man, a man in
>   all he is.

At first Tresckow's death was so well camouflaged that it was believed he had been killed in a skirmish with partisans. His body was taken back to Germany and buried with military honors on the family estate of Wartenberg. But eventually all the lines of investigation into the assassination attempt pointed to him. Sometime around the middle of August, the SS came to dig up and dispose of his corpse; Tresckow's widow and his daughters were already either in prison or in a foster home.

Helmut Stieff was one of the first arrested and put to death. On July 20, fearing that the attempt would fail, he had acted in a way that was not in accord with the second part of Operation Valkyrie: his indecisiveness had marked him as guilty. Betrayed by his contradictions, he was tortured and had confessed but pointed the finger only at people who were already dead. He was executed on August 8, hanged with one of the piano strings that had prolonged his suffering under torture.

Hans-Ulrich von Oertzen, whose role was to take over an area of Berlin, was arrested two days after the attempt and interrogated by the military. He was only twenty-nine and had been married for four months. He managed to telephone his young wife one last time, and then, knowing that the Gestapo would arrive at any moment, he pretended that he had to relieve himself, locked himself in the toilet, put a grenade in his mouth, and pulled the pin. His guards heard the explosion and found his poor decapitated body amid the debris of the door they smashed in. Heinrich von Lehndorff—one of the men who had witnessed the massacre at Borissov— was arrested the same day. Sentenced to death on September 3, he was hanged the day after, leaving behind a wife and four children. On July 26 it was Wessel Freytag von Loringhoven's turn to commit suicide. This forty-four-year-old colonel had provided explosives, which had been discovered. At the same time, Georg Schultze-Büttger was taken into custody. He was hanged on October 13, 1944, a few days after he had turned forty.

On August 17, 1944, Fabian von Schlabrendorff was arrested. Tortured at length by the Gestapo, he did not give us away. "The Boeselager brothers? No, they're excellent soldiers, completely loyal. They had nothing to do with it. You're wasting your time," he claimed. Under torture, his legal training came out. He raised procedural issues, and during a hearing he objected to the illegality of the treatment meted out to prisoners. Two of his ribs had been broken in interrogation; he created turmoil in the courtroom by displaying his injury. The prosecution was taken aback, and the trial had to be suspended. Then Schlabrendorff had a real stroke of luck: the courthouse was bombed, and his judicial dossier was lost in its ruins, along with the presiding judge, the infamous Roland Freisler, who had been carrying it. Asked afterward why he had been arrested and than interned, he replied that he was accused of "illegally slaughtering cattle." He was put in a concentration camp and then transferred, along with General Franz Halder and former French prime minister Léon Blum, to South Tyrol. After being freed by American troops, he returned to civilian life and resumed his work as a jurist; in 1967 he was appointed to the German constitutional court (Bundesverfassungsgericht). He died in 1980.

The day Schlabrendorff was arrested, Field Marshal Kluge was relieved of his command. Too much evidence showed that he had known what was going on and had covered for his subordinates: he was virtually condemned. On his way back to Germany, the old soldier committed suicide. He wrote a last letter to the Führer, begging him to stop the war, and declaring his fidelity for the last time. Despite these warnings, the war continued to chew up lives, families, and whole cities. On August 15 it was our dear Wilhelm König, our king of steel, who lost his life. Having survived incredible dangers, as if invulnerable, he was killed in an absurd way. One evening as he sat at his work table, he was hit by a stray mortar shell.

Every day, the mail brought us new reasons to mourn. Every day, official information reported the progress of summary trials. Hitler was undertaking a systematic purge. The repression spread, extending even to those who had only guessed what the conspirators were doing. Thousands were interned, sometimes for vague relationships with the members of the conspiracy. The military institution had to submit. Political commissars were named for the armies.

On July 24 the old military salute was abolished and replaced by the Nazi salute. Langen, the secretary of the

First Squadron of the Thirty-first Cavalry Regiment, received Göring's order on the subject by telephone; it was effective immediately. He typed up the verbal directive and presented it to the commander of the brigade straightaway. It was important enough to warrant interrupting the officers' work session. Georg was conducting a major briefing with the commanders of the two regiments, the battalions, and the squadrons. Langen, an NCO, knocked at the door: "Colonel, may I come in?"

"Yes, what is it?" Georg asked.

Langen entered and, following the new orders regarding military discipline, clicked his heels and gave the Nazi salute. The officers were appalled. In normal times, they might have smiled or thought it was a joke in poor taste. But in the context of the failed coup d'état, there was nothing to smile about.

"What is wrong with you? What does this mean?" Georg asked severely, showing a degree of irritation that was unusual for him.

Without a word, Langen handed him the paper. After rapidly perusing it, Georg asked, "Langen, from whom do you usually receive your orders?"

"From you, Colonel, and from the officers of our regiment, naturally," the NCO replied sheepishly.

"Good, Langen, you've understood. You may go," Georg concluded more kindly, with a slight smile.

The secretary backed out of the room after giving a very martial, and very classic, military salute. The directive was not followed in the brigade. A political commissar was named, but he was a former Communist full of contradictions, and showed no particular zeal in exercising his office. Moreover, he quickly became the butt of jokes within the brigade.

On August 8 I was named head of the Forty-first Regiment of the Second Cavalry Brigade, whose commandant had just been seriously wounded. I said good-bye to my brother, my childhood companion, without suspecting that death was soon to separate us forever.

"How many times in the course of this war have I prayed to God to take my life and preserve that of others whom I consider more important than I am! He has not listened to me, because apparently I have not yet passed my qualifying examination in the great beyond," Georg wrote in a letter to Annarès von Wendt in September 1942. Now Georg had passed his exam. He had shown that he could follow his convictions through to the end. In a certain sense, he was prepared to die. Georg was killed in combat on August 29, 1944, on the border of East Prussia—the Bug River near Lady-Mans. While he was driving along a ridge from which he was radioing directions to his troops, his vehicle was targeted by enemy mortar fire. He had just celebrated his twenty-ninth birthday. His participation in the conspiracy remained a secret. Georg's body was taken back to Heimerzheim—this was unusual in the context of the complete collapse of the military situation—and he was given a formal funeral.

*August 2, 1944: Georg presents the Iron Cross First
Class to his brother.*

A Time for Mourning

When Georg died, I lost half of myself. Tresckow, Hidding, König—all the members of the conspiracy whom I knew were dead. I was the only one still carrying the secret, without anyone to confide in.

But operational necessities left me no time to weep. Every day a new Russian attack nibbled off a few more kilometers. We were defending ourselves inch by inch, but we had to face facts: the Red Army would soon be at the gates of East Prussia. In the second half of August, the forces under my command, which were at that time retreating toward the west near Bialystok, began to move north, toward the border of East Prussia, and provided a clearly marked target for the Soviets.

In late August, I was summoned to army headquarters. A plane was supposed to take me there on September 1. This was clearly a trap to take me into custody; I was certain that my end was near. As I ran toward the waiting plane in a state of deep anxiety, my traveling Bible dropped out of my poorly closed bag and fell open. I bent down to pick it up, and saw these lines of the Benedictus: *Ut sine timore, de manu inimicorum nostrorum liberati, serviamus illi.*[3]

I regained my confidence and boarded the plane, saying to myself, "By the grace of God!"

21

The Bridge over the Mura

1945

It was not a trap that awaited me at army headquarters, but an appointment as special officer for the cavalry. I thus became the staff's correspondent for all matters connected with the mounted cavalry, and responsible for equipment and for the distribution and numbers of these troops, whether regarding the two brigades of mounted cavalry, the cavalry units attached to reconnaissance battalions for infantry divisions, the cyclist units, or the cavalry training school. I received requests from the operational units, and dealt with them in coordination with various administrative entities. I frequently visited the front lines in order to forge my own opinion concerning the most difficult points. The rest of the time I was located, like a large part of the infantry staff, in the offices of the former school of athletics in Wünsdorf.[1] Even though the town was rarely bombed, this period nonetheless induced anxiety. Not allowing myself to confide in anyone, to avoid aggravating my situation or endangering those with whom I might have spoken, I expressed myself freely only with my orderly. The atmosphere of feigned camaraderie among the staff was rather overdone; everyone watched what he said, while avoiding a reserve that would have been suspect. But I sometimes found it too hard to contain my feelings.

I had been invited by General Wilhelm Burgdorf (Hitler's aide-de-camp and the head of his personal office, who, at that time, called the shots at headquarters) to an after-dinner wine tasting. There were many generals there, and I was by far the youngest guest. Toward the end of the evening, as I was getting ready to go, I heard Burgdorf say in the next room, "When the war is over, we will have to purge, after the Jews, the Catholic officers in the army."

I went into the room, and after thanking him in the usual way, I said, "As a Catholic officer, I found what you just said very informative, General. I'd like you to know that despite my flaws, I have served the German people at the front, I have been wounded five times and been awarded the Iron Cross." There was an embarrassed silence, and without staying any longer I politely took my leave.

As for my new assignment, while I was sorry to give up operational functions and leave my men to their fate, I gained an overall view and an influence that I had never had before. I quickly became convinced that despite the distance, I could still be indirectly useful to my men. Over the following months, I had only one preoccupation: to save as many cavalrymen as I could. Until October my former companions in arms were used in inappropriate ways, broken up into minuscule units in extremely lethal trench warfare on the border of East Prussia. The number of horses at their disposal declined drastically. My visits in the field confirmed my worst fears: with the rapid advance of the Red Army, East Prussia was in danger of being surrounded, and the troops protecting it were threatened with complete annihilation. I wanted to get my comrades out of this wasps' nest, and to do so I counted on the Führer's craziest plans. For the end of 1944, Hitler envisaged a gigantic offensive far to the south, through Romania, in order to capture the oil fields in the Caucasus. The cavalry, which was very mobile, was ideally suited to this kind of operation: that was the argument I did not hesitate to use in order to move my cavalrymen to a less dangerous theater of operations.

Colonel von Bonin was at that time head of the operations division of the Army General Staff; he supported my plan. In addition, through the intermediary of his orderly, I had General Heinz Guderian's ear. On November 28, 1944, the Third Cavalry Brigade received its evacuation order and left a front where it had lost, in less than two years, 46 officers and 850 NCOs and enlisted men, and suffered more than 3,600 wounded. It took the last trains to get out of East Prussia: no less than fifty-six convoys to transport men, equipment, and horses. During the second half of December, the troops arrived in Hungary, near Lake Balaton, amid vineyards, ancient churches and abbeys, and manor houses from the Austro-Hungarian period. This rolling landscape was particularly cheering after the rigors of the devastated Russian plain. But the Soviets were already there. The Führer's offensive was no more than a madman's dream, and we could hope to do no more than delay the enemy's advance.

When I was finally able to rejoin my beloved cavalrymen, the Red Army was already at the gates of Austria. In the meantime, I had been promoted to the rank of major, and I was put in command of the Thirty-first Cavalry Regiment. I was welcomed with a joy that did my heart good, despite the difficulites that still faced us.

The news of Hitler's death reached the troops on May 1, 1945. It was met with general indifference, even among his former supporters; for months, everyone had been thinking only about getting home alive. My sole concern was to ensure that the boys who had been entrusted to me would return to Germany. Until the last day, I had all the infirmaries in the region searched for the division's wounded and amputees, in order to spare them from being massacred should the sector be taken over by Tito's partisans or by the Red Army. I did the impossible, right under the noses of the Russians, whose drunkenness helped me get three wounded officers out of the Juden-burg Hospital.

I heard about the surrender on the night of May 8, 1945, when the cavalry division had just finished its last hunting party of the war—and of its history. We had to make the right decisions, because the surrender did not mean the end of hostilities. The Russians were taking advantage of this unstable period to seize as much terri-tory as possible. Our regiment was supposed to cover the retreat of the whole cavalry corps, whose first units had crossed the Mura, south of Graz, on May 7. On May 9, shortly after midnight, at the rear of the cavalry corps, I myself crossed the bridge at Wildon. In the moonlight, I stopped my horse for a moment and went over to the parapet. Plunging two fingers into the lining of the left pocket of my uniform jacket, I pulled out the little cyanide capsule that had been with me for almost three years. Kluge, whose son-in-law was a physician, had given it to me one day when our airplane was almost shot down by partisans. Now I threw it into the river. Thus, this symbol of the painful end of my youth, of those years of bitterness and dread, of unspoken fears, sank silently into the water. This poison capsule was death itself, caught in a fold of my garment. I felt lighter. The war was over. I was alive!

But this was no time for dreaming. The roads were crowded with cars, trucks, and armored vehicles of all kinds. I had the bridge blown up at 4:30 a.m., in order to

Philipp in May 1945.

slow the Russians' advance a little. In Wildon I demanded that the mayor immediately burn the red flags adorned with the hammer and sickle that the inhabitants, who had two months earlier been supporters of Germany, had been cowardly enough to hang from the windows of their houses. When evening came, we set up our head-quarters in the village of Weitenhof, where we rested. The Mura, more than eight kilometers away, marked the boundary between the Russian and the Allied zones. We thought we were safe there, but we were mistaken. We had hardly settled in before my driver shouted, "The Rus-sians are here with tanks!" We immediately evacuated the village, the staff cars roaring off right in front of the stunned Russians, and we took the road to Köflach.

When we were some distance from the town, the head of the column called me on the radio: "Major, the English are in front of us. What should we do?"

"Well, say hello to them!"

I went up to the head of the column in order to meet my British counterpart. The introductions were cordial. We exchanged cigarettes. I told the Englishman that the Russians were occupying Graz. "Don't you want to help us drive them out?" he asked in jest.

"No thanks, frankly. Since the surrender, my job is to take my regiment back to Paderborn in Germany."

To escape the crowded roads and at the risk of run-ning into the Russians, we branched off to the west, and led by a guide, took a mountain road. It was there that we had arranged to stay when the English accepted our capitulation on May 11. We were supervised by cavalrymen, or rather former cavalrymen who had been transformed into tank men.

The countryside was splendid, and nature seemed to have prepared herself carefully to welcome our exhausted soldiers and provide them rest. The solemn setting of the Alps, the pine forests, the flourishing vegetation in full bloom—everything contributed to give the surrounding mountains an unreal appearance. The fighting, the gunshots, the machine-gun fire, the attackers' wild cries, and the death rattles of the dying quickly became memories. After having lived in the depths of hell, we were now near heaven. Game was abundant—roedeer and woodcocks delighted hunters. We had to find activities to occupy men who suddenly found themselves with nothing to do: I took volunteers on long rambles on horseback high into the mountains, we organized equestrian tournaments, Roman chariot races, and even acted out the rape of the Sabines in period costume. We were not taken prisoner or even completely disarmed. By July I was home again, my pistol in my belt and flanked by my two horses.

Epilogue

One day in October 2003, I received a letter from the office of the French minister for European Affairs, inviting me to a meeting with members of the French Resistance that was to be held early in the following year, in the presence of a few hundred secondary school students. On the occasion of the sixtieth anniversary of the invasion of Normandy, France also wanted to highlight the sixtieth anniversary of the assassination attempt made on July 20. The presence of the last witness of the resistance to Hitler among the German military was supposed to serve the cause of Franco-German friendship.

I accepted on the condition that I not be given a starring role. I was only the last representative of those whom fate had treated less generously. I therefore insisted on being accompanied by Henning von Tresckow's daughter, General Kurt von Hammerstein-Equordt's daughter, and Hans Oster's daughter-in-law—who herself had been arrested in April 1943 for collaborating with the lawyer Müller, who was conscientiously passing information to the Allies through a religious pipeline. The meet-

July 9, 2004.

Epilogue

ing took place on January 27, 2004, in a setting filled with sinister memories: the Foreign Ministry's Kleber International Conference Center in the former Hotel Majestic, whose cellars had been used to torture members of the Resistance. On the platform with me were Jacques Baumel, Marie-Jo Chombart de Lowe, Jean Gavard, Lucie Aubrac, and also Uta von Aretin, and Anna Oster. It was a very moving moment for me.

Moreover, France had reserved for me an unexpected honor: I was made an officer of the Légion d'honneur, as a posthumous homage to all my companions, and to Tresckow in particular. This gesture, carried out by France's minister of European affairs, was full of great symbolic value. The next day, I went to the Arc de Triomphe to lay a wreath on the Tomb of the Unknown Soldier. This was a kind of vengeance taken on cruelty and incomprehension for a man like me who had always tried to follow three rules: to keep my political conscience awake, to respond to the call, and also to know how to say no.

July 20, 2004: Philipp with his wife, Rosy,
at the Ploetzensee Memorial in Berlin.

Afterword

Shortly before the beginning of the offensive against the Soviet Union in 1941, Antonius and Georg von Boese-lager, along with my grandfather Karl von Wendt,[1] made a friendly pact: if one of them died during the war, the others would somehow find a way to bring his body back to Germany. This strange agreement soon had to be put into effect, alas, when Antonius died during the first weeks of the conflict. In November 1941, when Georg sent Karl von Wendt to look for warm clothing in Germany, he asked him to make a detour to Welish: under cover of night, he was supposed to disinter Tonio and take his body back to Heimerzheim. Karl did not demur; he did what was asked of him. When he arrived in Heimerzheim in the middle of the night, he dug a grave in the castle's private cemetery and buried the body.

In August 1942 Karl in turn died during the violent fighting around Rzhev. Georg, who was then in Romania, could do nothing. Then, starting in January, he was too occupied with the reorganization of the cavalry. He therefore entrusted the operation to Philipp, who was still Field Marshal Kluge's aide-de-camp. Philipp had the staff's carpenter construct an oblong box lined with zinc, which was supposed to protect his maps from the damp. The explanation seemed plausible enough; the box didn't really look like a coffin. Accompanied by his orderly, Philipp went to the cemetery where Karl had been buried. It was toward the end of the winter. Time was limited, because the Russian pressure on Rzhev was increasing again, and the region would no doubt have to be abandoned, along with its cemeteries containing many of their comrades. The two men went as far as Grubewo, five kilometers from Rzhev. The incessant combat over the winter had transformed the country-side into a lunar landscape. Of the city, which had formerly contained fifty-seven thousand inhabitants, there remained only ruins. That night, they went into the cemetery. The cross atop the tomb, with its inscription still perfectly legible, rose over a thick layer of snow. They brushed the snow off the tomb, but the ground was completely frozen. They had to sprinkle gasoline on the ground and set it on fire. It was a strange sight—these flames flaring in the quiet of a snowed-in cemetery, amid the silent population of ghosts! Philipp and his orderly didn't linger. They transferred the body to the map box, locked it, refilled the hole, and left. A few days later, Rzhev fell into Russian hands.

However, neither Philipp nor Georg had time to return to Germany. The military situation was poor.

Philipp's new responsibilities did not allow him to go on leave; therefore, he kept the body with him. The box was equipped with handles that made it easier to load on trucks. During sedentary periods, the mysterious container was unloaded and put in Philipp's lodging or his tent. He traveled for no less than eighteen months with Karl's body, which was finally buried only in mid-August 1944, by his brother-in-law Kaspar von Fürstenberg, a few days after Philipp took command of the Forty-first Cavalry Regiment. Philipp's efforts made it possible for us to rediscover my grandfather's remains and take them home to Germany in August 1997.

Florence Fehrenbach

Notes

CHAPTER 1

1. This residence was sold to the municipal government in 1923.

CHAPTER 2

1. Although the republican constitution secularized education, primary education remained under the de facto supervision of the clergy.

CHAPTER 4

1. I did not personally experience this episode, because at that time I was several hundred kilometers away. But my brother told me about it. Moreover, the following sequence has been described in the Sixth Division's journal of operations.

CHAPTER 5

1. The Eighty-sixth Division's movements were, after the sickle-shaped sweep toward the English Channel, part of the German

General Staff's other great strategic maneuver intended to cut up and disorganize the French defense.

CHAPTER 6

1. Karl von Wendt, an officer under Georg's command, comments on the attitude of the French people he had been able to observe in the town where Georg was in charge: "What is most surprising is that in both their behavior toward us and in their way of life, there was no sign that the French had lost the war to us. In the long run, they will finally realize this. It is equally strange to see so few people mourning, even though we can assume that every family has sustained a loss. However, we hear many people say that they are in captivity in Germany. But since these prisoners provide very favorable reports regarding the manner in which they are treated in Germany, the population is very friendly and helpful to us. People never cease to go into ecstasies over the fact that we are very decent boys, and they do not hesitate to express very clearly their admiration for our army. In particular, they are astonished by the quality of our discipline, and they put the blame for their defeat wholly on the poor leadership of the French armies." (Florence Fehrenbach, *Un coeur allemand: Karl von Wendt (1911–1942), un catholique d'une guerre à l'autre* [Toulouse: Privat, 2006], p. 138.

2. This is once again corroborated by Karl von Wendt, Georg's faithful battalion chonicler, in a letter written to his wife on July 20, 1941, in the heat of action: "The Russian people reject this war more and more as we advance, and themselves call the Russian Army 'Bolsheviks,' with whom they have no relationship. In many places we see people bringing their crosses and icons out of hiding places; many of the prisoners display religious medals to prove their good faith when we ask whether they are Bolsheviks. Hardly a day goes by without people among the civilian population, usually older people, telling us that communists are still hid-

ing in the forests. Obviously, we can't go running after every one of them, but I think the civilian population is 70 percent on our side. In particular, when they have lived a few days alongside German soldiers and have been able to see that we aren't killers and brigands like the Reds, who behave in a truly crazy way within their own country. In the long run, the Russians would be able to maintain that kind of regime, and the game will soon be up for the Reds who are holding power. May the Lord be merciful if they fall into the hands of this people whom they have persecuted for twenty years now. The few cities and towns that there are here are now being systematically burned by the Reds, but that does not harm us or put us in danger, only it will take the country a long time to rebuild itself." (Ibid., p. 236.)

CHAPTER 7

1. These were 75 mm mortars, adapted so that they could be pulled by horses at a trot. They had a limited range.

CHAPTER 8

1. Since 1938, Oster had been risking his life in an effort to bring together undecided generals in order to lead them to undertake a putsch and prevent a war that would be disastrous for Germany. The Abwehr had understood this as early as the mid-1930s, because the country did not have the resources to sustain a long war (a replay of its situation in 1914). Several times, Oster had purely and simply committed treason, handing over to the Western powers information regarding war plans and communicating to the Dutch military attaché on May 8, 1940, the date the offensive was to begin.
2. Letter to Anna-Therese Freifrau von Wendt, October 5, 1942.
3. Letter to Anna-Therese Freifrau von Wendt, October 12, 1942.

Notes

CHAPTER 9

1. In 1924 Bach-Zelewski had been expelled from the Reichswehr because of his pro-Nazi sympathies. After half a decade of struggling to survive in one job after another, he received a large inheritance. He joined the Nazi Party in 1930 and the SS in 1931, and he became a deputy to the Reichstag in 1932.
2. In 1942 Bach-Zelewski fell into a deep depression that left him on the verge of madness. He both conceived and organized the battle against partisans, and he was also an advocate of recourse to "the most brutal means." On this subject, see J. L. Leleu, *La Waffen SS* (Paris: Perrin, 2007), pp. 788–95. We can imagine that Kluge at least suspected what kind of man he was dealing with.
3. Bach-Zelewski died in 1972, after ten years in prison.
4. Stargard (in Polish, Starogard) had been given to Poland in May 1920 along with the Polish Corridor, and was reincorporated into Prussia in November 1939 after the destruction of Poland.

CHAPTER 10

1. The Wolfsschanze, near Rastenburg in East Prussia, is the best known and the best organized of the different general headquarters. The one in Vinnytsya, Wehrwolf, was used from July to October 1942.

CHAPTER 11

1. Böhne was an estate belonging to Field Marshal Kluge's wife.

CHAPTER 12

1. Bernd von Kleist was then an administrative officer on the staff.

Notes

CHAPTER 13

1. The story told by the noncommissioned officer Heetmann expresses the admiration and even affection that his men felt for their leader, which is also proven by the use of Georg's nickname: "Yes, our Schorsch [Georg] is coming to visit his good old squadron. We all like him and venerate him, and we would follow him into hell. We can hardly control our impatience. While waiting, we've all gathered, some at his post, others in front of his bunker. No one is cold, despite the Siberian cold, because our Schorsch is going to arrive. And then, suddenly, like a hunter on the lookout for game, there he is in front of us, accompanied by our King of iron and steel. He smiles at us, shakes our hands, and talks to us the way a father talks to his children. He knows how much we are suffering, he knows that things are going badly for us. He talks about the future. Everything is silent, we hang on his every word. He is going to get us out of here and put together a cavalry group. At the mere thought of that, all the cavalrymen's hearts swell in their breasts. Then he shakes everyone's hand again, wishes us good luck, and bids us farewell." (Quoted by Hans-Joachim Witte and Peter Offermann, *Die Boeselagerschen Reiter: Das Kavallerie-Regiment Mitte und die aus ihm hervorgegangene 3. Kavallerie-Brigade/Division* [Schild Verlag, 1998], p. 23.)

CHAPTER 17

1. After the war, Hans Herwarth von Bitterfeld became the German ambassador in London and a secretary of state to President Heinrich Lübke.
2. It is impossible to say with certainty whether it was these explosives that he used in the following days. It seems, in fact, that Stauffenberg had explosives that came from at least four different sources, only two of which were discovered by the Gestapo. The

precautions taken at every step of the way prevented the investigators from reconstituting the whole sequence.

CHAPTER 19

1. Hidding was finally interred about August 16, 1944, a month after his death, along the road to Jedrejzow, at the same place as the grandfather of Florence Fehrenbach.

CHAPTER 20

1. Major Kuhn survived his captivity in Russia, but returned to Germany in very poor condition.
2. Born Erika von Falkenhayn, she was the daughter of the German commanding general at the battle of Verdun in 1916; he was later defeated by the British in Palestine in 1917. Since his leave in 1943, she had been aware of what her husband was doing.
3. Luke 1:74: "that we, being delivered from the hand of our enemies / might serve him without fear."

CHAPTER 21

1. On the outskirts of Zossen, since 1908 the town of Wünsdorf had been the home of an army training center, which became the army's official School of Athletics in 1924.

AFTERWORD

1. On Karl von Wendt (1911–1942), his life, and his correspondence, see Florence Fehrenbach, *Un coeur allemand* (Toulouse: Privat, 2006).

Bibliography

ON RESISTANCE WITHIN THE GERMAN MILITARY

Hoffmann, Peter. *German Resistance to Hitler.* Cambridge: Harvard University Press, 1988.

Thun-Hohenstein, Romedio Galeazzo. *Der Verschwörer: General Oster und die Militäropposition.* Berlin: Severin und Siedler, 1982.

ON HENNING VON TRESCKOW

von Tresckow, Henning. *Ich bin, der ich war.* Berlin: Lukas Verlag, 2001.

ON GEORG VON BOESELAGER

Doepgen, Heinz W. *Georg von Boeselager: Kavallerie-Offizier in der Militäropposition gegen Hitler.* Herford, Germany: Mittler, 1986.

ON ARMY GROUP CENTER AND THE SIXTH INFANTRY DIVISON IN PARTICULAR

Grossmann, Horst. *Die Geschichte der Rheinisch-Westfälischen 6. Infanterie-Division 1939–1945.* Bad Nauheim: Hans-Henning Podzun Verlag, 1958.

Haape, Dr. Heinrich. *Endstation Moskau 1941–1942.* Stuttgart Motorbuch Verlag, 1998. (A very detailed and lively account of the beginning of the Russian campaign, written by the physician of the Third Battalion of the Eighteenth Infantry Regiment of the Sixth Division. With maps and illustrations.)

Bibliography

ON THE GERMAN CAVALRY AND THE BOESELAGER BROTHERS

Witte, Hans-Joachim, and Peter Offermann. *Die Boeselagerschen Reiter: Das Kavallerie-Regiment Mitte und die aus ihm hervorgegangene 3, Kavallerie-Brigade/Division,* Munich: Schild Verlag, 1998.

ON THE ATTITUDE OF A NONCOMMISSIONED OFFICER DURING THE RUSSIAN CAMPAIGN

Fehrenbach, Florence. *Un coeur allemand: Karl von Wendt (1911–1942), un catholique d'une guerre à l'autre.* Toulouse: Privat, 2006.

Kageneck, August von. *Examen de conscience.* Paris: Perrin, 1996.

———. *Lieutenant de Panzer.* Paris: Perrin, 1994.

Illustration Credits

7   Philipp and his siblings in front of the family house. © Collection Boeselager.

9   Philipp, nine years old, with his father's hunting trophy, September 1926. © Collection Boeselager.

23 Berlin, September 1938: parade of the Paderborn Fifteenth Cavalry Regiment honoring Mussolini. © Collection Boeselager.

58 January 1942, Hitler's headquarters at Rastenburg, East Prussia: decoration of (from left to right) Hans Jordan, Karl Eibl, Günter Hoffmann-Schönbron, Georg von Boeselager, and Karl-Heinz Noak. © Ullstein Bild.

67 Headquarters of Army Group Center, summer 1942: Philipp, sitting; Captain Bülow, standing. © Collection Boeselager.

73 Kluge's office at Smolensk. © Collection Boeselager.

75 Departure of the Army Group Center general staff for a tour of the battlefield (September 1942). © Collection Boeselager.

77 July 1942: Kluge on the battlefield; Philipp is at right. © Collection Boeselager.

Illustration Credits

116 The officers' dining room where the March 1943 attempt to shoot Hitler was to take place. © Collection Boeselager.

128 Operations briefing, Russia, July 1943. © Collection Boeselager.

144 With Lieutenant Schulte, at Patrykozy (fifteen kilometers north of Second Army headquarters at Petrikov), 1944. © Collection Boeselager.

165 The two brothers with their comrades from the Third Cavalry Brigade. © Collection Boeselager.

167 Tresckow, Georg, and Oertzen. © Collection Boeselager.

174 August 2, 1944: Georg presents the Iron Cross First Class to his brother. © Collection Boeselager.

181 Philipp in May 1945. © Collection Boeselager.

185 July 9, 2004. © AFP (Agence France-Presse).

187 July 20, 2004: Philipp, with his wife, Rosy, at the Ploetzensee Memorial in Berlin. © AFP (Agence France-Presse).

Index

Page numbers in *italics* refer to illustrations. Page numbers
193–198 refer to notes. Page numbers in *italics*
followed by *n* refer to footnotes.

Abwehr, 62, 98, 103, 195
Aloïsius Jesuit secondary school,
    10–11, 19
Alsace and Lorraine, 14
Amsberg, Major, 111–12
Aretin, Uta von, 186
Armament, Ministry of, 139
Army General Staff, German,
    81, 99, 111, 178
    Organizational Department
      of, 110
Army Group A, 27, 31
Army Group B, 27
Army Group Center, 65, *67*, *75*,
    83, 85, 108, 113, 118, 123,
    127, 133
    casualties in, 151
    Gigas's provisions of supplies
      to, 155, 161
    more soldiers needed by, 139
    Philipp in, 71, 72, 74, 76

    Soviet frontal attack against,
      150
Army Group South, 98, 123,
    127, 145
atrocities by Germans, 21–2,
    79–82, 97, 98, 123–4
Aubrac, Lucie, 186
Auer (soldier), 31–2
Austria, 20

Bach-Zelewski, Erich von dem,
    76, 78–81, 82, 196
Bassewitz, Captain, 126
Baumel, Jacques, 186
Beck, Ludwig, 99, 168
Belov, Pavel, 108
Berghof, 152
Berg-Schönefeld, Carl-Friedrich
    von, 99, 102
Bettermann (artillery
    commander), 123

Index

Bismarck, Gottfried von, 110

Bitterfeld, Herwarth von,
141–2, 197

Blomberg, Lieutenant, 53

Blum, León, 170

Bock, Fedor von, 83, 98

Boeselager, Albert von, 4,
13–14, 19–20

Boeselager, Antonius von, 8, 14,
26, 29, 41–2, 189

Boeselager, Georg von, ix–x, 12,
15, 46, 47, 68, 85, 94, 110,
115, 123–4, 126, *128*, 148,
167, *174*, 194

  birth and childhood of, 3–6,
  7, 8

  in burial pact, 189, 190

  in cavalry, 17, 18, 22, *23*, 24,
  25–6, 28–9, 30, 31, 35–7,
  38–9, 40, 41–3, 48, 49,
  51–2, *56–7*, 59, 62–6, 106,
  107–9, 110, 111–12,
  129–32, 134–7, 151–2

  as commander of Third
  Cavalry, 163–4, *165*, 172

  death of, 173, 175

  decorated by Hitler, 57, *58*

  education of, 16–17, 61

  in French invasion, 28–30, 31,
  35–6

  Hitler criticized by, 64–6

  hunting by, 4, 5–6, 8, 112, 164

  illness of, 62–4

  Kluge's meeting with, 108–9

  models for, 107–8

  nickname of, 197

  in occupation of France,
  35–6, 194

  in Operation Valkyrie, 153,
  154, 157–8, 160, 170

  Paris trip of, 150–1

  in push for Panther Line,
  134–7

  in Soviet invasion, 38–9, 40–1

  on Tereben mission, 129–32

  wounding of, 137, 138–9,
  143, 146–7

Boeselager, Hermann von, 8

Boeselager, Philipp von, *75*, *77*,
128, *144*, *174*, *185*

  at anniversary of plot, 184,
  186, *187*

  Army Group Center
  presentations by, 74

  atrocities condemned by,
  79–82

  atrocity prevented by, 123–4

  birth and childhood of, 3–6,
  7, 8, *9*, 10–11

  in burial pact, 189–91

  in cavalry, 16–17, 18, 22, *23*,
  24, 25–6, 31, 33–4, 40, 52,
  53–5, 129–32, 134–7, *165*,
  176–80, *181*, 182–3

  childhood incident with SS,
  14–15, 87

  in conspiracy meetings,
  101–2

cyanide capsule carried by,
180
education of, 10–11, 14–16,
18, 61
explosives studied by, 101,
140–1
in French invasion, 31–4
Galen and, 69–70
Hitler criticized by, 61–2
on Hitler's offer to Kluge,
91–4
hunting by, 4, 5–6, 8, 96
as Kluge's aid-de-camp, 68,
71, 72, 74, 87–8, 89–93, 97,
117–18, 190
national service of, 18–19
in occupation of France, 35
in Operation Valkyrie, 153–5,
157–8, 159–61, 170
plot against Hitler revealed
to, 93
in push for Panther line,
133–7
religion of, 6
in Soviet invasion, 40, 41
on Tereben mission, 129–32
at Vinnytsya meeting, 85–8,
89
wounding of, ix, 52, 54, 55–6,
57, 58, 59, 71, 74, 138, 141,
143, 146–7, 177
Boeselager Reiterverband, 112
Bonin, Colonel von, 178
Bormann, Martin, 85–6, 87

Brandt, Colonel, 119, 120
Breitenbuch, Eberhard von, 166,
168
Brest-Litovsk, 156, 157–8, 160,
161
Brinckmann, Major, 162
Bülow, Captain, 67
Burgdorf, Wilhelm, 177
Busch, Ernst von, 146–7

Canaris, Wilhelm, 98
Casablanca Conference, 103
Chombart de Lowe, Marie-Jo,
186
Clemens August, Prince-
Archbishop of Bavaria, 3
Commissar Order, 43
Congregation of Mary, 15–16
Cuno, Chancellor, 13

Deecke, Dr., 137
Deutsche Jungvolk (Pimpfen),
15–16
Doege, Lieutenant Colonel,
33–4
Dovator, Lev, 107–8

Eibl, Karl, 58
Eighty-sixth Infantry Division,
26, 31, 37–8, 85

Fifty-eighth Infantry Regiment,
40
First Boeselager Battalion, 132

Index

Forty-first Cavalry Regiment,
191
Fourth Army, 27, 133, 138, 151
France, 12
    advance into Germany by, 26
    German advance into, 27–34
    German occupation of, 35–7,
    194
    Rhinelanders' prejudice
    against, 13
    Russian invasion of (1812), 42
Freikorps, 78
Freisler, Roland, 170
French Resistance, 125, 184, 186
Fürstenberg, Kaspar von, 191

Galen, Clemens August von,
69–70
Gavard, Jean, 186
Gersdorff, Rudolf von, 32–3
    in plot, 99, 114, 120–1
    resistance joined by, 83
Gestapo, 169, 170, 197
Gigas, Lieutenant, 137, 138, 155,
161
Godesberg, 6, 10, 15
Goebbels, Joseph, 120
Gollert-Hansen, Captain, 155
Göring, Hermann, 120, 121,
152, 172
Great Britain, 12, 103
    German capitulation
    accepted by, 182–3

German invasion planned for,
37
Great Depression, 107
Guderian, Heinz, 178
Gypsies, 76, 79–80

Haape, Dr., 63–4, 65
Halder, Franz, 81, 170
Hammerstein-Equordt, General
von, 184
Hardenburg, Carl-Hans von,
82–3
Heetmann, Officer, 197
Heimerzheim, Germany, 3–4, 6,
10, 21, 108, 147, 150, 173,
189
Helldorf, Count, 110
Heroes' Day, 120
Hidding, Lieutenant, 146, 158,
161, 175, 198
Hill 208, 135–6
Himmler, Heinrich, 86, 118, 152
Hirsch, Major, 37, 38, 46
Hitler, Adolf, ix, 14, 61–2, 64,
68, 81, 177, 178
    accession to power by, 19
    death of, 179
    Georg decorated by, 57, 58
    Kluge's conversations with,
    89–91
    offer to Kluge by, 91–4
    Operation Citadel launched
    by, 127

purge undertaken by, 171
Smolensk abandoned by, 133
on Soviet front, 151
T4 program halted by, *69n*
Ukrainian diplomats ordered
   shot by, 83
World War II tactics of, 81
Hitler, Adolf, plots against, ix, x
   bomb on plane, 119–20
   bomb plot at Berghof, 152
   coup d'etat planned for
      aftermath of, 118, 121, 140,
      152, 172
   first aborted attempt,
      118–19
   Gersdorff's bomb plot,
      120–1
   and improvised tribunal, 117
   meetings on, 101–2
   motivation for, 103–4
   Philipp's learning of, 93
   planned shooting, 113–15,
      116, 117
   rumors of, 110
   Stauffenberg's attempts at,
      152–3
   Tresckow's early thoughts on,
      97–8
   war as obstacle to, 125–6
   see also Operation Valkyrie
Hoffmann-Schönbron, Günter,
   58
horses, 105–6, 111, 126–7, 134

Höxter, 101
Hungary, 179

Imperial Guard, 97
inflation, 13

Jägerhöhe, 142
Jews, 79–80, 82–3, 123–4, 177
Jordan, Hans, *58*
Joseph, Archduke of Austria, 86
Judenburg Hospital, 180
Jungstahlhelm, 15

Kageneck, Franz-Josef von, 48,
   49, 51, 64, 65
Kalinin, Russia, 44–5, 48
Kant, Immanuel, 64
Keltsch, Dr., 137
Kleber International Conference
   Center, 186
Kleist, Bernd von, 99, 196
Kluge, "Hans" Günther von, *73,*
   75, 77, 78, 97, 111, 196
   on Army Group Center's
      requirements, 139
   and atrocities, 123–4
   in automobile accident, 138
   Bach-Zelewski's conversation
      with, 79–81, 82
   frontline visited by, 74
   Georg's meeting with, 108–9
   Hitler's conversations with,
      89–91

Index

Kluge, "Hans" Günther von
  (continued)
  Hitler's offer to, 91–4
  initial assassination attempt
    called off by, 118–19, 121
  and Operation Citadel, 114,
    127
  Philipp as aid-de-camp to, 68,
    71, 72, 74, 76, 87–8, 89–93,
    97, 117–18, 190
  Philipp given cyanide capsule
    by, 180
  plot against Hitler approved
    by, 102–3, 109, 117–18, 120
  Smolensk's abandonment
    pushed by, 133
  Tresckow's plan rejected by,
    151
  at Vinnytsya meeting, 85–6,
    87–8
  western front command
    taken by, 150
König, Wilhelm, 108, 111, 117,
    147
  in Operation Valkyrie, 158,
    171, 175
Köstring, General, 141–2
Krebs, Major General, 93–4
Kristallnacht, 21–2
Kuhn, Major, 164, 198

Langen (secretary), 171–3
Lehndorff, Heinrich von, 82–3,
    169–70

Les Andelys, 27
Lippert, Rudolf, 22
Loringhoven, Wessel Freytag
    von, 170

Mit brennender Sorge, 19
Model, Walther, 85, 120, 166
Moritz (horse), 127
Morrell, Theodor, 119
Moses (Heimerzheim Jew), 21
Müller (lawyer), 184

Nagel, Second Lieutenant,
    43–4
Napoléon I, Emperor of the
    French, 40
Nazis, 18, 19–20, 80, 96, 110
  Aloïsius Jesuit secondary
    school and, 11
  Bach-Zelewski in, 196
  Georg's criticism of, 65
  Philipp's criticism of, 61
  power assumed by, 12
  youth organization of,
    15–16
  see also SS
Ninth Army, 38, 48, 85, 87, 151
Noak, Karl-Heinz, 58
Normandy, invasion of, 149–50,
    184

Oertzen, Hans-Ulrich von, 97,
    100, 167, 169
Olbricht, Friedrich, 100, 152

Index

110th Infantry Division, 51

126th Infantry Division, 51

186th Reconnaissance Battalion, 31

Operation Citadel, 114, 127

Operation Valkyrie, 140, 145, 152–62, 163
  deaths in aftermath of, 166, 168–73
  sixtieth anniversary of, 184, 187

Orel-Briansk panhandle, 127, 129

Oster, Achim, 62

Oster, Anna, 186

Oster, Hans, 62, 69–70, 98, 100, 103–4, 118, 168, 184, 195

Paderborn Cavalry Regiment, 17–18, 25

Panther Line, 133, 134–7, 138

Papen, Franz von, 110

Pétain, Philippe, 32

Pimpfen, 15–16

Poland, 81

Pretzell, Major, 99, 100

Propaganda, Ministry of, 155–6

Reichskommissariat Ost, 74

Reichstag, 196

Reserve Army, 152

Rodewyck, Father, 15

Romania, 59, 66, 94, 178, 189

Ruhr, 13

Rzhev, 51, 52, 57, 84, 87

Salis-Soglio, Baron von, 17–18

Schlabrendorff, Fabian von, 98–9, 100, 117, 119, 120, 152, 170–1

Schmidt-Salzmann, Walther, 112, 115

Schmundt, Rudolf, 113, 114

Schulenburg, Fritz-Dietlof von der, 112

Schulte, Lieutenant, 144

Schulze-Büttger, Georg, 97
  in plot against Hitler, 99, 100, 104, 170

Second Army, 145, 152, 153, 154, 163, 166

Second Battalion, 134

Second Cavalry Brigade, 173

Second Cavalry Corps, Soviet, 108

Seelen, Father, 13

Sicherheitsdienst (SD), 74, 123, 124

Siegfried Line, 26

Sixth Cavalry Squadron, 26

Sixth Infantry Division, 26, 27, 37, 38, 39, 40, 42, 47, 48, 50, 51, 151–2

Sixth Reconnaissance Battalion, 38, 46, 63, 85

Smolensk, 73, 132–3

Index

Soviet Union, 37–45, 46–57,
       103, *128*, 129–31, 143,
       145–6, 149, 163–4, 179,
       180, 194–5
   atrocities against Jews
       prevented in, 123–4
   barbarism in, 122–3
   German front under attack
       in, 49–54, 84–5, 107–8,
       131–9, 150–2
   German invasion of, 37–40,
       189
   German positions abandoned
       in, 132–3
   Graz occupied by, 182
   horses on German front in,
       105–6
   Operation Citadel launched
       in, 127
   Panther Line in, 133, 134–7,
       138
   Romanians in, 59
   SS's authority in, 74, 76,
       78–81, 123, 124, 146
   temperatures in, 46–7, 48,
       49–50, 53
SS, 118, 146, 196
   atrocities by, 78–81, 123–4,
       146
   authority in Soviet Union of,
       74, 76, 78–81, 85, 123, 124,
       146
   Philipp locked in closet by,
       87, 88

   Philipp locked in garage by,
       14–15, 87
   Tresckow's body dug up by,
       169
Stahlhelm, 14
Stalin, Joseph, 43
Stargard, 81, 196
Stauffenberg, Claus von, 142,
       152–3, 159, 164, 168
Stieff, Helmut, 101, 110, 140,
       141, 142, 169
Stolberg-Stolberg, zu, 8, 10

T4 program, 69
Tereben, 129–32
Thiedemann, Fritz, 112
Third Cavalry Squadron, 130–1,
       146, 155, 163, *165*, 178
Third Panzer Army, 151
Third Squadron, 158
Thirty-first Cavalry Regiment,
       153, 157, 172, 179
Tito, 179
Tresckow, Erika, 168, 198
Tresckow, Henning von, 65–6,
       68, 72, 74, 82, 95–6, 112,
       113, 114, 152, *167*, 184
   assassination conspiracy and,
       92, 99–100, 101–3,
       104, 119
   atrocities condemned and
       prevented by, 97, 124
   on cavalry, 109, 110
   death of, 166, 168–9, 175

Index

Georg's meeting with, 109
and Gersdorff's suicide plot
 to bomb Hitler, 120
on Hitler's offer to Kluge,
 92–3
in Operation Valkyrie, 140,
 145, 153–4, 159–60
piety of, 96–7
post-assassination plan of,
 150–1
recruits to conspiracy made
 by, 99–100, 102–3
resistance joined by, 83
Tereben mission ordered by,
 129
Twenty-eighth Chasseurs
 Division, 164

United States, 47, 103, 133

Verdun, Battle of, 198
Versailles Treaty, 18
Vinnytsya, Ukraine, 84–8, 89,
 118, 196
Volga, 42, 44, 48, 49, 51
Voroshilov, Kliment, 45
Voss, Alexander von, 100

Weimar Republic, 12, 20
Wendt, Annarès von, 173
Wendt, Karl von, 47, 189, 190,
 191, 194, 198
Wöhler, General, 72, 74, 75
Wolff, Baron von, 147, 148, 152
Wolfsschanze, 113, 140, 196
World War I, 8, 13, 15, 21, 78
World War II, ix, 25–6, 60, 62, 93
 casualties in, 107, 151
 see also France; Soviet Union

Printed in the United States
by Baker & Taylor Publisher Services